THOUGHTS OF A BOY GROWING UP

THOUGHTS OF A BOY GROWING UP

By Kenneth E. Nelson

Goodluck, Annijke!
Ken Nelson

Founded 1910
THE CHRISTOPHER PUBLISHING HOUSE
HANOVER, MASSACHUSETTS 02339

COPYRIGHT © 1999
BY KENNETH E. NELSON

Library of Congress Catalog Number 96-86565

ISBN: 0-8158-0525-x

PRINTED IN THE UNITED STATES OF AMERICA

Dedication

This book is dedicated to my seven wonderful grandchildren, Brandon, Alexandria, Zachary, Kenneth, Justin, Blake, and Darren, who so often asked, "Grandpa, tell us about when you were a boy?"

The account that follows is an attempt to do just that, in a chronological fashion.

My memory may be faulty in laying down a sequence of events in the correct order.

Where my three brothers, Roy, Don, and Harold, are mentioned, they might quite properly challenge the accuracy of activities involving them.

Overall it is my best account of events and feelings likely encountered by many other youths growing up in the era of "barefoot boy with cheeks of tan." I must admit I never learned to whistle.

Contents

Our Mountain School	1
Endless Experiences	13
Learning About Birds and Animals	27
Learning About Adults	45
Our Family Moves To Town	63
We Become Dairymen	71
Ray Union School and Miss Potter	85
Changes and More Changes	93
My Brother Leaves	105
Tragedy on the Farm	117
Sports, Woodshop and Graduation	123
After Graduation	135
Girls and A Kayak	145
A Vacation; I Become A Sailor	155

Left to right, the author, Kenneth E. Nelson, his brother Roy Nelson, Mildred Lindley, Jack Smith (all four in the same grade) and Leland Hadley, one grade higher in the Upper Mattole School.

Foreword

The Nelson family seemed to me to live a truly pioneer life that demanded hard and monotonous work with little respite. In this large family everyone contributed to the providing of food, shelter, and sociability. The effort of every family member was needed, was expected, and the responsibility was accepted.

Today we frequently hear about the lack of responsibility on the part of our young people and how nice it would be if we could only go back to those wonderful pioneer days when there was something constructive for our youth to do. Many of the perceived ills of our society would surely vanish.

One also hears that "all work and no play makes Jack a dull boy." I always marveled that the Nelson siblings somehow managed to either make some tasks fun or to play a little between chores. As Ken's cousin I often visited him or stayed overnight and I saw that for Ken it became an accepted challenge to find time to do things he wanted to do. There was never a lost moment and this carried on in life after he became an adult.

Our society talks of the value of "character" and I have to believe that living the pioneer life is one way to successfully build "character". The amount of work demanded of the pioneer and the responsibility expected of the individual would be sobering to most people today who often fantasize over the curative value of such a life.

Bruce B. Black

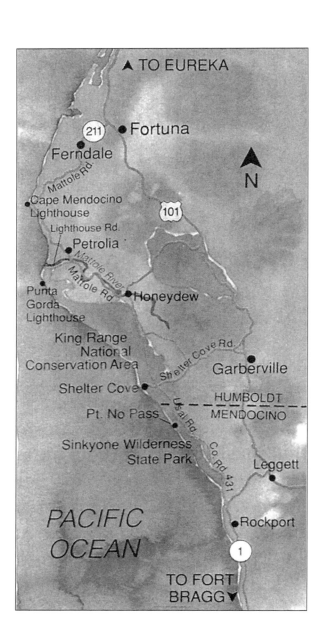

Our Mountain School

My earliest childhood memories must date back to about 1926, when I was not yet six years old.

School began for me when I was 5½ years old. Because going to school meant walking on a dirt road for over a mile and a half, my parents had my brother, Roy, wait until he was seven, so we could start first grade together.

Our mother walked with us to school that first day. We must have been excited although I don't remember my feelings. Both of my younger brothers were born by then. Our father must have stayed with them. It could have been our grandparents (my father's parents, who lived in a big house on a mountain an hour's drive away).

You can picture the three of us walking up on the school porch, opening the door, and our mother telling Miss Cartwright, "These are my two boys, Roy and Kenneth."

School was underway when we arrived. Nine other students were sitting at desks or around tables. Miss Cartwright smiled and said, "Hello, Roy and Kenneth. Why don't you sit down at this table? There are tablets and crayons, or clay if you would like to make things with it."

My brother, Roy, was ready. He had been ready for a year! Very soon he was engrossed with "school" and totally at home with the other younger children.

My only response to Miss Cartwright's second request to join Roy at the table was to cling more tightly to my mother's legs. I didn't want anyone to see my face. I was scared! Both the teacher and my mother seemed to understand. It was suggested that my mother walk me home and come back again the next morning. Roy was agreeable to staying the balance of the day at school.

I guess that my mother had the strength and endurance that only mothers have. She later walked back the mile and a half again to accompany Roy home. He must have convinced me that school was all right as I stayed through the following day.

I don't remember ever disliking school, but having a brother in the same class who always understood directions better and usually did better, was a little stressful. Both of us did well, though, at the little one-room school.

Miss Cartwright, and the young teacher who followed her, Miss Moll, always spent a half-hour reading to the students. Having a story that continued each day soon became one of the best parts of school. Looking back I marvel at how Miss Cartwright and Miss Moll were able to select books that appealed to all of the different ages of their students.

Only one small piece of a story stays with me: it somehow had to do with boys hiding apples, for what purpose I don't know. Roy and I couldn't wait to get home. There was a big barrel of apples in our woodshed, with straw placed between the apples to cushion them and to prevent rot from spreading.

One by one we removed the apples from the barrel and hid them around the woodshed and the adjoining room where the machine for making apple cider was kept. It also served as a toolshed. After having been entranced by Miss Cartwright's story what we did made great sense to us.

Fortunately, before rats or other rodents discovered many apples, my father noted the almost-empty apple barrel. He knew who to ask! I remember our feeling "dumb" in trying to explain the reasoning for disturbing the family's winter supply of apples.

Our school had no piped-in water. Probably there was a container of water inside the school building, with a dipper.

Separate boys and girls lavatories were located in opposite corners of the schoolyard. They had standard holes cut into the board that served as seats. A Wards or Sears mail-order catalogue provided paper.

Near the girls' lavatory was an upside-down faucet, serving as a fountain when turned on. Water came from a spring on the hillside.

* * * * *

Outdoor games at our school, as young people know them today, were almost unheard of. We didn't play baseball, soccer, basketball or any other organized games.

Often during summers after lunch, we walked to the Mattole River that was close by, waded in the shallow water and chased tiny trout, or sat at a sandy part of the river's edge and built sand houses. Sometimes we boys caught water dogs, lizard-like things with red, leathery skins, who hid under water but couldn't swim fast enough to escape us.

Sometimes we climbed the fence on the edge of the school yard and took sleds up the steep hill for exciting rides downhill on the dry grass. Roy and I had an advantage in building sleds. The boards that my father shaped to stretch, "grain" and dry animal skins became wonderful "runners" for the wooden sleds.

No doubt we thought about playing kick-the-can or kick-the-wicket, but the only tree in the school yard was a single big maple tree on the west side of the school building. There weren't many places to hide.

In those days in the Mattole River Valley we went to school all summer, except for a two or three week break. The 2-3 month vacation came during winters because the heavy winter rainfall made travel almost impossible. Bridges in low areas washed out regularly. Tractors, cars or teams of horses had to be called on to pull stalled cars out of overflowing creeks that covered many roads several feet deep.

We children found it terribly exciting to watch the streams of muddy water flowing along the sides of our road and tearing away the dirt and small gravel.

The heavy rains and horrible lightning and thunder frightened my mother. The threat of quite regular sharp earthquakes made things worse. My father was a "mountain man." He saw no reason to be frightened, though that didn't allay my mother's fears. Some of us children buried our faces and ears into pillows. I'm not sure what I did, but being extra brave didn't describe me.

Our house was a single-walled building that didn't keep out all of the winds or rain. The kitchen was at one end of a long, main room, with a big kitchen stove. A wood-burning heating stove was along the outside wall at the end of the room away from the kitchen. Doors led from the main room into two bedrooms, a pantry and the bathroom.

During each winter most of the buckets and pans our family owned were used to catch drips from the ceiling. No one seemed to consider this unusual.

Our house had something some of the homes in the Mattole River Valley didn't have, a flush toilet and a bathtub. The family who owned the ranch before us had run a two-inch iron pipe from the house up to a location in the creek about one quarter of a mile up the hill. The sections of the pipes were connected with rubber inner tubes from old tires. We had lots of water pressure except when winter storms knocked down trees and tore the water pipe sections apart. I remember many times when my father braved the storms with spare inner tubes, wire and pliers, to make sure our house had running water.

Who used the bathtub? I guess my mother and father did though I never remember them bathing in it during the seven years we lived there. I often saw my mother washing clothes on a washboard in the tub.

Hot water was available only after the wood-burning kitchen stove had been burning for half an hour. For continuous hot water, the fire in the stove had to be kept burning, even during summer days. I can remember my mother filling a portable metal tub with nice warm water in the kitchen end of the house, for us children's weekly bath.

Without electricity, kerosene lamps were the only source of light. I'm certain there wasn't a lot of nighttime reading done by anyone. Once in a great while a drop of water would hit a lamp chimney and cause it to explode in pieces. My mother was always fearful of this happening and of flying pieces of glass destroying an eye of one of her family.

My father bought and tried one of the newest sources of light then available, a Coleman lamp, using extra clean gasoline and a mantle. For a few seconds when he lighted up these new devices the house would be filled with unbelievable light, but then the mantles would crumble into ash and we would be back to the light from the wicks of the kerosene lamps. Electricity was never brought to our area while we lived there.

* * * * *

Summer was extra nice at school. The teacher let us students sit under the big maple tree for lunch. She was just like one of us, it seemed.

I remember Miss Cartwright as being very pretty. Some of the local farm boys must have also thought this was true.

Once, during lunch under the maple tree, a young man on a horse came galloping across a field next to the school yard. I don't remember his first name, but his last name was "Roscoe," a well-known family name in our community. As the rider got near the four-foot wire fence around the school yard, it became apparent that he intended to jump his horse over the fence. How better could he impress this young woman teacher?

But the horse had other ideas! When it reached the fence the horse planted its front feet and stopped dead in its tracks. Its rider was thrown over the fence into the school yard.

After the initial shock and seeing the rider get to his feet, all of us students began to laugh. I think our teacher was awfully embarrassed. In later years I came to realize that kids laugh at some things that aren't funny at all.

* * * * *

When I was six or seven, my grandfather and grandmother moved from their house up on the mountain top several miles away to a pretty forested area just across a bridge from us but still on my parents' ranch.

Over a period of two years they built a campground with eight or ten cabins, and finally a nice new home for themselves. Almost every day when we weren't in school, my brother and I would be watching the construction going on. It was fascinating to watch the cabins take form.

My grandparents were very stern. I don't remember them ever laughing. They were nice, though. They lived for about a year in the first cabin they built. When all of the cabins were completed, they built a quite large home for themselves.

My brothers and I would often, on weekends, walk over to their cabin in the mornings. Even though we may have had breakfast, they always had a couple of pancakes and maple syrup for us, and maybe just a tiny piece of bacon. What a treat!

My grandfather always walked with a limp. A horse had kicked him in the leg when he was younger. It never completely healed and he kept a patch over the semi-open wound. The infection must have gotten into his leg bone. I know we felt sorry for our grandfather because it had to hurt, but there wasn't anything we could do to help.

* * * * *

The Mattole River encircled about half of our ranch. During winter the water ran up to thirty feet deep and huge logs were dragged all the way to the ocean. Big chunks of our ranch land crumbled down into the roaring waters. Roads occasionally had to be moved back from the steep banks.

During summer it was a small river and in places you could wade across it as you still can today. Although winter rain totals are among the highest in the United States, summer is very dry and the water is warm and good for swimming.

Our mother was fearful of us going near the river. We had absolute orders not to go to the river alone. I don't remember us ever violating those rules.

My brother Roy and I were allowed to play in the little nearby creek almost whenever we liked during summer, although much of summer was spent in school. I'm certain my mother worried about us slipping on the rocks in the creek, and hurting ourselves, but she never refused to let us go there.

That little creek was an endless place of wonder for us. We built dams, canals and waterfalls. We captured the little frogs and "skeeters" that seemed to be everywhere. Because we were always barefooted, we never had to keep track of shoes and sox. If we didn't roll up our trouser legs far enough, pants soon dried out in the warm sun after we climbed out of the creek.

No one understood the truth better than my brother and me of there being music in little creeks. Once the water slowed to a trickle during summer, there was endless musical notes coming from the water flowing over and around the rocks and into tiny pools. We never tired of listening to the hundreds of wonderful sounds coming from that little creek.

When our grandparents had finished building most of the cabins, they would take time out to go trout fishing in the Mattole River during summers. There weren't large trout, just five to eight inch long young steelhead.

Occasionally our parents would allow Roy and me to walk down to the lower part of the ranch where our grandparents liked to fish.

The river had washed in under the low banks and the trout liked the deeper water there. The trees often hung out over the water.

I remember when I was seven or eight, Roy and I were watching our grandparents fish. They were fishing about one hundred feet apart, off the bank. We would walk back and forth hoping to see a fish caught.

All of a sudden the limb my grandfather was leaning on broke and he fell into the deep water. Every time he came to the surface, I yelled, "Grandpa, should I get Grandma?" About the third time, he managed to grab a root and pulled himself up on the bank. For a year afterwards my grandfather teased me about asking him if "I should call Grandma," but doing nothing about it. Neither my brother or I could swim, nor could my grandparents.

* * * * *

Mostly I felt awfully good at school with no memories of older students being anything but helpful to us younger ones. I remember both of our teachers, Miss Cartwright and later on, Miss Moll, as being always kind and fair. With so few students everyone got any help they needed to make certain the work was understood. Grades at our school were in "percentages." I had never heard of A's, B's, C's, etc. or S (Satisfactory), O (Outstanding) or U (Unsatisfactory). Letter grades were to come later after we moved to Lodi for the fourth grade. We liked bringing home report cards showing most subject grades as 80s or 90s.

Clean ears and fingernails aren't high priorities for two mountain boys plodding a mile and a half to school each day on a dirt road. Too many interesting things along the road needed to be picked up and examined, and rocks needed turning over. What started from home in a clean condition didn't always arrive at school that way.

Our teacher encouraged clean hands, necks and ears with a little positive reinforcement project. Each student was assigned an "animal" cut out of cardboard. These were started together each semester in the chalk trough, and a hundred or so even spaces marked out on the bottom edge of the blackboard.

Every morning on arrival, each student was carefully examined for clean faces, hands, fingernails, etc. Our "animals" were moved according to our scores. It's possible that one of us boys won the "cleanliness race," but the one or two girls probably took most years by a wide margin.

Our lunch pails were empty lard buckets. One or two students came from families who could afford the luxury of a purchased lunch box. Our lunches consisted mainly of a sandwich and a small glass container of milk, plus a piece of fruit if plums or apples were in season.

Without ice or refrigeration, the milk was air temperature and stayed that way. I didn't especially like milk except on cereal or as part of a bread and milk supper.

One day at school I was told I didn't even pronounce milk correctly. Other students claimed I said "malk" and I guess the teacher agreed. It was decided that I should practice. Our teacher asked everyone to close their eyes while I said "milk," not "malk." It was a disaster; I was mortified. After trying it once or twice to no one's satisfaction, I gave up saying that word at all except at home. My mother said it sounded all right to her.

I guess tempers must have gotten out of hand occasionally. One day, for some reason, I hurled a rock at a schoolmate, Jack, and hit him in the forehead. Miss Moll lost no time in sending me home, after severely scolding me for doing such a dangerous thing. That probably was one of the longest walks I ever made. My mother just couldn't understand why I did a thing like that.

Jack's younger brother, Tom, already had only one remaining eye because of a children's bow and arrow incident in their family.

Endless Experiences

My father must have believed without question that he could make a living for his family from farming the 365 acre mountain ranch he was trying to buy during the 1920s. He sent to agricultural research stations for numerous pamphlets on growing wheat, vetch, apples, sheep, pigs and cows. My father was an excellent student, having graduated from high school with honors.

His first and largest venture was wheat growing. Most of all I remember the plowing, harrowing, planting and the summer harvest. My parents had two big, reliable horses who could pull a single-bottom plow for hours at a time. My brother and I liked to walk in the furrow behind the plow and marvel at the worms turned up by the plowing. A flock of birds soon discovered the feast and followed the plow throughout each day.

After a year or two, my grandfather helped my father purchase a single cylinder John Deere tractor. What a marvelous machine it was! It could pull almost anything. You could hear the "Pop, Pop, Pop," as the tractor moved across the field, taking the place of our two horses, and my father riding in a seat rather than walking. Plowing and harrowing could be done in a quarter of the time.

Grain harvest took on a sort of community effort. Summer campers from my grandfather's flourishing "Camp Nelson" would volunteer to help my father during the ten days of wheat harvest.

My father hired a couple of local young men to help. One I remember especially because he seemed to like my brother and me, and of course we took advantage of that. His name was Russell. After a day's work he would take his blanket and pillow and lay everything out for sleeping on the edge of an old straw pile in the meadow behind my grandparents' campground.

My brother and I would show up about bedtime and take turns grabbing either Russell's pillow or blanket, and then tearing around the straw pile, with poor Russell in hot pursuit. We never tired of it, but Russell eventually told my father he had to get some sleep for the next day's work. Fathers can sometimes sure take the fun out of things.

One day after lots of hours of pulling in the piles of wheat on sleds and wagons to the stationary harvester, my father suggested a swim in the river to clean off the dust of a day's hot, sweaty work.

It was a great idea! We climbed down the steep trail to the river's edge and all of the men stripped naked. In they went into that warm, wonderful fresh water. My father asked me if I wanted to climb on his shoulders and go into the river. I jumped at the chance!

Unfortunately, my father was only ten feet into the river when he stepped off a rock ledge into a deep hole. Under both of us went! It was frightening as I couldn't swim. Fortunately my father quickly recovered and got me back to shore, coughing and still pretty shaken. I declined any further offers to go into the river.

* * * * *

It never would have occurred to me during the ten days of wheat harvest that my mother enjoyed her role — that of preparing a magnificent lunch (the main meal) for the harvest crew, usually 5-6 men. Always there were big dishes of fried meat, mashed potatoes with all that wonderful gravy, dishes of fresh-cooked vegetables, and always pies, enough for "seconds."

It was only many years later that my mother confided that those harvest days were wonderful for her, with the knowledge that all those workmen enjoyed her meals so much. Too, it was adult company not often found in that remote country. My mother never did drive and was rather isolated at home with her large family, eventually five children.

Occasionally she visited mothers on their nearby ranches. One situation required walking across a swinging footbridge spanning the Mattole River. Though a frightening experience, my mother apparently braved it just for a two-hour visit with this neighbor.

Another woman friend lived a mile away. This walk included climbing through a barbed-wire fence, and across a cattle pasture, with the always threat of bulls.

* * * * *

My brother and I were totally fascinated by wild animals on the ranch, whether it be squirrels, mice, skunks, deer or scary thoughts of panthers and bears. When wheat was cut, shocked and stacked for drying before being put through the harvester, mice always found a home under the stacks of curing wheat.

Nothing was more exciting to Roy and me than catching the mice that scurried around when the piles of cured wheat were lifted by pitchforks onto the sleds or wagons. Our several cats just loved to eat mice. Each wagon or sled had an old coffee can nailed onto it. We put the captured mice, when killed, into the cans for the hungry cats.

One time I had my hand in a "mouse can," checking to see how many mice we had captured, when the horses started to move the wagon to the next stack of wheat. The sharp edges of the can sliced into my forearm deeply and ended my fun for that day.

The infection, impetigo, set into the wound and my parents had a very difficult time getting my arm to heal. It must have taken several weeks to heal and left a permanent inch-long scar.

The pieces of straw blown out of the harvester during separation of the grain, was later hauled to the winter hay barn. A special piece of machinery was operated to blow this "chaff" into the barn. Someone was needed to use pitchforks and move the straw back from the spout so it wouldn't pile up and choke off the incoming flow of material.

My brother and I, at seven or eight years old, were assigned the dusty job of standing close to the incoming blast of chaff. With the big forks we moved the incoming straw back out of the way. I can't forget trying to keep up with the incoming avalanche of straw and crying because the dust was so choking. It was an awful situation with no escape! It was the one part of each summer wheat harvest that I feared.

The barn full of chaff had little value for animal feed. It was kept in mangers for the sheep and cattle during winter months. They nibbled on it occasionally.

Chaff piles were no playground at all. The itching that followed walking through it seemed to last for hours.

For bedding material, chaff was usable and effective. Both the sheep and cows welcomed a layer of dry material to lie on, although it soon became punched into the under layer of mud.

* * * * *

Squirrels were as fascinating to us as were the mice. My father had dozens of single-spring steel traps and double-spring traps to catch fur-bearing animals for their pelts. Roy and I could "set" the smaller, single-spring traps by ourselves. Ground squirrels aren't welcome in the mountain communities. They eat the grain, walnuts, hazelnuts and anything else that appeals to them. My brother and I were "heroes" when we trapped and killed a squirrel.

Every day one summer, on the way to school, we would climb through the ranch fence alongside the road and check our squirrel traps. We had set them in a shallow ditch cut out in the wheat field by water from heavy winter rains. It was easy to find the squirrel runways as they traveled from their burrows to the feeding areas. Traps were set in the runways, hoping an unwary squirrel would step on the trap's "pan" and set off the trap. We covered the pan with a light cover of dry grass so the animals wouldn't sense trouble before it was too late, and a paw was firmly held by the steel trap jaws.

One morning we had success! A squirrel was held fast with a front paw in the trap. It didn't seem particularly concerned and I grabbed it firmly behind its head while Roy and I opened the trap. For some reason I decided to take the squirrel to show to our teacher. Maybe I was going to put the squirrel in our teacher's top desk drawer to surprise her. That doesn't sound fair to a teacher, but maybe I thought it was a great idea to watch her surprised face.

I held the squirrel tightly behind it's head, and off Roy and I went to cover the last mile or more to school. On the way we sometimes met an older girl, Dorothy, and her younger brother, Orville, and walked on to school with them. Dorothy and her family lived in a little cabin in the woods a few hundred feet off the main road. We knew they were very poor, but the family was sort of a mystery. It was rumored that the father had alcohol problems and didn't really support his family, and was often away. My parents asked that we not go into the woods to Dorothy's and Orville's place.

They met us that morning and were properly impressed with my squirrel. Dorothy immediately wanted to carry the squirrel for a while. I was proud of having that little wild animal and didn't want to chance losing it, so I refused. But Dorothy was older and very insistent. Eventually her pleas wore me down and I reluctantly handed her my squirrel. She agreed to grip the squirrel exactly as I showed her.

Her grip around the back of the strong little animal's head wasn't exactly right. The squirrel saw his chance and promptly bit Dorothy's hand. She instinctively flung the squirrel away. The freed animal raced across the road and scooted up a tree. I don't exactly remember what I said to Dorothy, while trying to hold back tears, but I'm sure it had something to do with the "inferior side of girls," and no doubt was pretty unfair.

Rattlesnakes, too, were quite often seen during summer months while on our walks to and from school. The thought of rattlesnakes terrified our mother, especially with doctors and hospitals being several hours away. Roy and I, even at seven or eight years old, respected rattlesnakes but never let one get away, once it was sighted slithering across the dirt road as we walked along our way.

It took a dozen or so well-thrown rocks and soon each rattlesnake was bruised so badly that it couldn't escape. We would finally kill the snake with a long stick and then place a big rock on it's head while we cut off the rattles. Our parents and our teacher couldn't help but be impressed with our "proof" but they constantly warned us to never get too close, even if the snake appeared dead.

On the way home from school the road dropped down into Kendall Gulch, with a bridge crossing the little summer creek. Going down into the creek was a pleasant interlude and a place to scoop up a handful of water to drink.

For a year or two we watched carefully for "blue-bellied salamanders," large lizards with a supposedly poison bite.

Finally we got up courage to catch one, tease it with a stick for a while to observe it's teeth, and how ferociously it bit the stick. It wasn't long before we were letting the salamanders bite our hands. It was no more than a "pinch" from the animal's tiny teeth.

* * * * *

Bird nests have always been a marvel to children everywhere, as they should be. On our way back and forth to school during the spring and early summer, Roy and I always watched the trees for signs of nest-building. Only one episode do I remember clearly. My parents had bought each of us a fine cap with a shiny, slick lining inside. I know they were so proud to have us wear those caps to school. They were the kind that men driving fancy, open sports cars wear. For some reason Roy and I didn't feel out of place wearing them. I'm not sure how these fine caps matched coveralls and bare feet.

On the way home one early summer day we decided to see what was in a nest in a maple tree alongside the road. My brother climbed the tree and announced that there were four fat baby birds in the nest. I asked that he hand them down to me so I could hold them for just a little while. The inside of my new cap looked like a wonderful "nest" for the baby birds and soon all four were struggling around in their new environment — my cap! Suddenly I noticed the baby birds were having bowel movements!

When I handed them back to my brother so he could gently place the baby birds back in their nest, I found the inside of my cap fouled with multicolored bird manure. Here I had ruined my cap the first day of wearing it! We walked down into a creek in a canyon further down the road going home, and tried to scrub out the stain, but with no success. Although the wetness dried in the inside of the cap, there was no removing or hiding the stain. My mother never made an issue of the bird manure stain in the cap, but I remember always holding it afterwards so none of the other school children ever noticed the embarrassing stain.

My brother and I did so many things together, and were so close that he never told anyone about my cap. It was sort of understood that many things had to be our secrets.

The road to school curved around a huge rock formation, likely eight to ten feet high and fifteen feet across the top. The rock had weathered for many thousands of years and soil covered most of it's top and sides.

During the early summer, "wild onions" and "wild lettuce" seemed to grow especially well on the sides and top of our favorite rock. The bulbs of the plants we called the wild onions were especially tasty and often further delayed our walk home.

* * * * * *

Big animals were mostly just hearsay, stories passed from one person to another. That wasn't true with deer and rabbits. They were regularly hunted by my father for meat.

But bears and panthers were talked about, and marvelous tales told, but with not much evidence. Occasionally we heard the "baying" of bear hounds in the distance. That was most exciting and something that made us children just a little bit apprehensive. Suppose a frightened bear came tearing down the road with those hounds behind him!

One afternoon a couple of men on horses came down the road past our house, leading a third horse with a dead bear across the saddle. The dogs trotted alongside. The horse loaded with the bear seemed awfully nervous. I remember us marveling at what great hunters these men must be. They seemed to sit extra straight as they passed our house.

One winter day a most exciting thing happened. Because money was so scarce and there wasn't any farming to do at that time of year, my father would select places up through the mountains, usually alongside creeks, to set steel double-spring traps, hopeful of catching raccoons, skunks, ringtail cats, civet cats, minks or otters. He would set the traps where these wild fur animals might pass and bait them with pieces of old meat.

Once the traps were set, my father would check his "trap-line" every day or two, regardless of how severe the weather was. It was important to remove the animals from the traps as soon as possible. Animal furs didn't bring much money during the early years of the depression, but some would sell for 50¢ or $1 if the skins were perfect and well-prepared. My father became very skilled at "graining," stretching and drying skins. We always waited with a lot of anticipation when he was due back from checking his trap-line.

One morning, after being away all night in the mountains, my father came walking down the trail to the house. He asked if he could borrow the red wagon that had been our main present the prior Christmas. He wouldn't tell us anything and wouldn't let us follow him back up the trail with our wagon.

In about an hour he came back with a big black bear tied to the wagon. My father explained that he had killed the bear with a single shot from the rifle he carried, when the bear, caught by only a couple of toes in the small trap, had jumped around a tree and startled my father as he approached the trap site. I guess a big black bear leaping up with a couple of "Woof! Woofs!" would startle the bravest among us.

All of us children were amazed and impressed. We had never seen a 200-pound bear up close, much less had one where we could examine it's teeth, fur, eyes and claws. My mother wasn't nearly as impressed. All she noticed was the smell and the fleas. It became worse because it rained steadily so the bear had to be skinned and dressed-out inside the house. I remember my father talking about all of the positive things, like where we were going to hang that magnificent bearskin and all of the good bear meat we were going to have for eating.

The bearskin covered almost an entire wall in the pantry. It hung there until the smell of rotting fat got so bad, my father reluctantly took the skin down. Although I have no memory of what happened, it certainly didn't become a fancy bearskin rug to brag about.

The bear meat? We must have eaten some for several days and then discarded the balance. My father wasn't for throwing anything away, but even he had to admit this particular bear meat wasn't the best tasting. As he explained, "The salmon and steelhead were spawning up the nearby creeks, and the bear had no doubt been feasting on the semi-rotting fish." My father assured us that if the bear had been taken earlier, after feeding on berries, roots and acorns, it would have tasted fine.

Apparently huckleberries are a favorite late summer food of bears. Our parents cautioned Roy and me to be wary when we climbed the hills to reach our favorite huckleberry bushes. It wasn't something we ever worried about. It was sort of a pain to have to select so many tiny berries to get a decent mouthful.

* * * * *

Getting prepared for winter eating for a big family took a lot of planning and hard work. I remember our parents spending hours with a deer carcass, cutting all of the meat off the bones and into small chunks. These were stuffed into dozens of quart glass jars. Water and some salt was then added until the jars were full and the meat covered.

Our parents had a huge iron pressure cooker that would hold twelve or eighteen one-quart jars. The cooker would be placed on the top of the hot cookstove and the top tightened down with bolts. Water was put in the bottom of the cooker, several inches deep. As the water in the cooker boiled and steam formed, pressure built up. Watching the steam pressure gauge was critical because a certain pressure had to be reached and held at that level for a specific amount of time, to insure complete cooking of the meat.

The steam pressure being built up in the cooker always seemed to make my mother a little nervous, especially when the needle got close to the red zone on the gauge. She occasionally asked my father if he was sure the cooker wouldn't explode, and insisted we children move way to the other end of the room.

At the proper time the big cooker would be lifted from the stove and the pressure inside allowed to slowly drop. The bolts would be undone, the lid lifted and the jars removed. It was important to screw the jar lids on tightly while very hot to allow cooling with a vacuum inside the jars of meat. The pantry soon had several rows of cooked venison. It was a good feeling to see all of the shelves filling up.

I remember seeing jars of other canned supplies filling the pantry shelves as the year progressed.

Our grandparents had a large cherry tree and some of those were canned. We had a fifty-foot long patch of Loganberries that overwhelmed us with fresh berries. Lots seemed to be left over for canning and berry jam.

My parents canned tomatoes, peas and green beans from a large garden. It seems I remember them constantly worrying a lot about the possibility of those canned foods ending up poison. I know they were awfully careful in the canning steps taken.

* * * * *

Salmon were another source of winter meat. Only once do I recall my father allowing Roy and me to go with him to the river to try for a salmon during the start of the spawning season.

Timing had to be exact. There needed to be enough rain to cause the river to raise and signal the fish that it was time for their winter run upstream. The river couldn't be too deep or the backs of the salmon couldn't be seen as they moved upstream through the shallow riffle areas.

My grandfather had always speared a few of these salmon for winter food and had specially selected ten-foot wooden spear poles. There was a U-shaped heavy metal piece attached to the end of the big pole. To these were fitted spear points with big barbs to prevent the fish from freeing themselves, once speared.

It was true excitement as we followed our father to the river and watched from the shore while he waded knee deep into the rushing, somewhat muddy riffles to wait for a salmon moving upstream. If things were perfect the backs of the big fish showed above the fairly shallow water.

Several times my father saw a fish making it's run upstream through the riffle and hurled the huge spear. Each time the salmon was out of reach or my father just plain missed. It meant pulling the long pole back with it's attached rope and again waiting.

Finally a 30-pound monster got within range and my father's heave found it's mark. I would never have believed a fish could be so powerful! Water was thrown everywhere as the big salmon tried to jerk free, but the barbed spear points and the rope held. It was a proud day to walk the half mile back to our house with such a catch. No one minded the rain.

Salmon meat for winter use was prepared and pressure-cooked the same way as venison. We very likely had salmon once or twice a week for dinner through the entire winter. I don't believe I ever tired of the taste. My mother didn't try to make special dishes with salmon meat. She just heated and served it as it came out of the quart jars.

My father must have honestly felt his family could "live off the land" on such days when he landed a salmon or carried home a big "buck" brought down by his expert marksmanship. Occasionally, it was one of my brothers or me who spotted a nice three or four point buck trotting across the road and up the gentle slope behind the barn! My father would grab his big rifle and it usually wasn't long before we heard the explosion of the single shot needed to bag that deer.

Learning About Birds and Animals

Except for a Christmas trip to Lodi to visit my mother's parents, I only remember one time we, as a family, went for a several day stay away from the ranch.

My uncle and his family ran a big dairy in a community called Ferndale, about a 60-70 mile drive from our place. They apparently had invited our family up for a visit. If there was a period of reasonable winter weather, we could get away because our school was out for much of each winter. It was decided to accept their invitation and we packed up for the several hour trip to Ferndale, including about a ten mile drive along the coast. I'm not certain my sister was born yet, but fitting even six people into the small Chevy touring car with supplies for a four-day stay had to be a major task.

Two of our older cousins, both boys, were regular helpers on the dairy. The two girl cousins, my age or younger, didn't get involved with the milking, but had major household chores.

What a surprise I had! My uncle and the two boy cousins were out of bed and off to the dairy barn at 2:30 every morning! Here I was thinking about all of the pleasant things we would do together! By 7:00 A.M. they were in for breakfast with the balance of the family and us.

All four children were off to school before 8:00 A.M. At 2:30 in the afternoon they were home and the two boys off to the milking barns as soon as they changed clothes. There was barely time to say "Hello" and "How was school?" My brother and I hardly found anything to do, though we likely played games with our girl cousins once they arrived home from school.

By 6:30 P.M. milking was completed, dinner was over and our boy cousins immediately went to bed — no talk, no games, just bed! After all, they had to be up and milking again by 2:30 the next morning.

One morning the family did get my brother and I up at 5:30. We desperately wanted to help this busy family somehow. Fresh carrots were a regular winter crop for these dairy animals. They had been planted so as to reach maturity during winter, when fresh grass wasn't plentiful.

A tractor with a small plow-like tool was used to root-up the carrots. Then the tractor was hooked to a wagon and the carrots, probably a ton of them, were thrown by hand onto the wagon. After getting to the barn the carrots were washed and fed to the waiting animals. The cows seemed to "go crazy" over the fresh carrots and devoured both tops and bottoms.

For my brother and me, it was a cold, wet, muddy, disagreeable hour pulling and throwing the carrots onto the wagon. I'm not sure we volunteered again! We may have, though, because we couldn't believe anyone worked so hard as our boy cousins did.

The visit was our first exposure to a 2-wheel bicycle. Roy and I noticed our cousins jumping on it and riding here and there without problems. We couldn't wait until everyone was off to school to see what we could do. My brother did better than me, but neither did well. For one thing, it was a full-sized 26" bicycle and we couldn't get onto the bike easily or reach the pedals at the down position. Even worse there was no system for coasting, nor any brake. When the wheels turned, the pedals went around. If we got going a little fast and then didn't hold our legs way up in the air, the turning pedals would knock us off the bicycle.

Dairymen in the community seemed to be divided between those of Portuguese decent and other family origins, like my cousins'. There must have been some friction between the groups though no one mentioned it to us.

One day one of my boy cousins came home early. When asked by my aunt what happened he said he had gotten in a fight with another student. Apparently the teacher had asked my cousin to apologize to the boy. My cousin said, "I told her I wasn't going to apologize to any G— D— Portagee." He had been sent home for that response. We had never been exposed to different cultures and were puzzled about the entire situation.

I know I returned home with a lasting respect for my aunt and uncle and cousins. It was difficult to imagine that their level of work went on every day of the year.

It was easy, though, for me to understand why they were rich and we weren't.

* * * * *

Another activity my brother and I really thrived on was climbing the mountain behind the barn on our ranch. It was really quite steep in places, but was no problem for two healthy, barefoot boys. Much of the mountain was open grass, some was covered with oak trees and evergreens.

When an oak tree was knocked down in a storm we would pull off great blankets of moss. These we used to build "tents" and pretend they were our houses. Nothing made better or softer carpets for the floors! We really surprised our mother by coming home dry after a short but heavy rainstorm caught us on our mountain. Our playhouse had kept us completely dry during the storm.

There was a place on the mountain our father called the "second opening" because you went from an open hillside area, through several hundred yards of forest, and then into another fairly small open grassy area.

For Roy and me, approaching the "second opening" always was cause for much anticipation and excitement. If we crept out of the forested area very quietly, there were occasionally deer to be seen feeding on the grass. If there was a buck among them, we couldn't wait to tell my father.

Roy and I often talked of going further than the "second opening" but always decided against it because of worry about meeting bears or panthers. Being brave only went so far.

One summer day we discovered a steep slide area in the second opening. There was no grass and the steep, hard surface was covered with tiny particles of rock. Once Roy showed the courage to slide down on his bottom, I was quick to follow. Before long we had each made a dozen exciting slides down the hard, gritty surface.

Then we discovered something else! We had worn off the seats of our coveralls. Two "pink cheeks," slightly scuffed, showed through.

We worried aloud all of the way back down the mountain as to how to break the news to our mother. She wasn't pleased at all but didn't punish us. She said she thought our coveralls could be patched. Most of our clothes already had patches on the knees. No one made an issue of patched clothing. Most of the boys in school had their share.

There was an immense ant hill located halfway up our favorite trail up the mountainside. We usually avoided it for fear of having dozens of biting ants up our pant legs.

One day we captured a two-foot non-poisonous snake and decided to find out who could win, the snake or the ants.

We gave the snake no chance, and held it down until the thousands of ants had the snake firmly anchored and helpless.

Roy and I were a little ashamed about what we had done and never told our parents, nor did that again.

* * * * *

Hazelnuts grew wild on our ranch. It didn't take us long to discover the half-dozen clumps of hazelnut bushes that were close enough to monitor.

The many squirrels kept even a closer watch on the maturing nuts than we did. Most years we would forget, for just a few days, to keep watch and then come back to find every hazelnut gone. They were carefully stacked somewhere for some squirrel family's winter food supply.

One year Roy and I did beat the squirrels to the hazelnuts. It meant picking the several pounds of nuts days ahead of them being fully ripe. But we beat the squirrels!

We carefully peeled back the long annoying prickly sheath around each nut, a job that in itself took several hours. Then we took a ladder and placed the nuts in a single layer on the low part of our barn roof. Roy and I each had an equal share and our own location. The idea was to dry the almost mature hazelnuts, and to have a hideout even the squirrels wouldn't find.

We would climb up to the roof each day and select several nuts for cracking to see if they were really ready to eat. The hazelnuts tasted great at any stage and were all eaten before getting completely dried and ready.

* * * * *

Chickens have long been a great source of food for farm families everywhere, particularly so in early years when markets weren't close by.

Our henhouse was a place to be visited everyday during the spring, summer and fall. Today's hens lay eggs regardless of the time of year because laying houses are constructed and lighted so the birds don't know what season it is.

I remember our chickens laying fewer eggs as early October came around. By then my parents had accumulated enough eggs to last much of the winter if we used them sparingly. Care had to be taken to make certain eggs weren't allowed to get warm. Most eggs were "fertile" because roosters roamed freely around the farmyard with the laying hens. Eggs that were allowed to be consistently warm for a period of time showed embryo growth, and weren't eaten.

Each fall about 100 eggs were set aside for incubating. The incubators were warmed by a small kerosene stove for the period required to produce the baby chicks. It took several weeks time for the chicks to hatch and peck their way out of their shells.

All of us children marveled at the transformation of normal-looking eggs into living, feathered baby chickens. We loved to watch them grow to where they could be turned loose and fed grain in a shed, and eventually given total freedom outside. They provided "fryers" plus a new generation of laying hens. The older hens became delicious boiled chicken dinners, sometimes the source of "chicken and dumplings."

One winter we tried out a material called "waterglass" to preserve eggs. It was a gelatin material that was dissolved in water. The solution was then poured over a several gallon crock filled with fresh eggs. When cooled, the waterglass became like heavy Jell-O. To use the eggs later they had to be dug out of the waterglass and the messy stuff scrubbed off the eggs.

Waterglass storage was supposed to keep eggs more fresh for a longer period of time by keeping air away from the eggs.

Stale eggs, four or five months old, never tasted as good as the fresh ones, and we were always happy to see the chickens begin to lay eggs again as early spring came around. We used the waterglass method for only one winter so it couldn't have worked much better than just keeping the eggs as cool as possible.

One afternoon in late summer, my brother and I crawled into the henhouse and carried out the ten eggs that had been laid during the day. Instead of taking the eggs to the house, we decided to carry them into the woods and do target practice at trees. I don't know why we thought the eggs wouldn't be missed and questions asked.

Roy and I took turns throwing an egg at a designated tree. It was such a challenge! I do remember how excited each of us was if we scored a direct hit, and saw the egg splatter all over the tree. I don't remember who won but I can't forget who lost!

Just as we were coming out of the woods, my father was walking towards us and asked, "What have you boys been doing?" Our response was a quite natural, "Oh, nothing."

My father walked into the henhouse to gather up the day's eggs. When he came out empty-handed, his second question was, "What did you boys do with the eggs?" There was no point now in denying anything. We led my father into the woods and showed him the egg-splattered tree.

His response was immediate. He reached up, broke a small branch off a tree, stripped off the leaves, and called us over in turn, for a good "switching." The chicken eggs were always safe after that reminder.

Smoking salmon was a regular early-winter activity on most nearby ranches, as it was on ours.

It seemed to take several days with a low-burning, smoky fire to properly smoke the slabs of fresh salmon. The smell was wonderful as was the taste later.

Though restrictions on catching the winter run of salmon were few, we never seemed to have enough of this delicious smoked meat to last very many weeks into winter.

* * * * *

Other animals earned our parents a little income and provided a lot of interest for us children. Most likely, the twenty or thirty sheep we had kept our attention the best.

During the hardest part of the winter, the flock of sheep spent a lot of time in their side of the big barn. My brother and I had the job of spreading the wheat straw and chaff from the summer harvest onto the dirt barn floor for bedding. It required repeating every couple of days during rainy periods.

During late winter most of the ewes gave birth to their lambs. Every morning Roy and I would rush out to see how many new lambs there were. Even mother sheep are almost always gentle, and didn't mind our presence.

Once in a while we came back into the house to report that a ewe was lying down "funny" and wasn't moving. My father would run out to see what might be done. Most times it was too late.

If the lamb survived, an effort was made to get another ewe to accept this orphan along with it's own. Sometimes that did work and soon the lamb's tail was shaking delightfully as it found it's first breakfast.

Sometimes it was necessary to feed the new lamb on diluted canned milk from a baby bottle to give it a chance for life. My mother was especially good at this and often the little lamb was up and around and constantly searching for more food. This may sound easy but all of these motherless lambs had to be bottle-fed until they could join the other sheep feeding on the early spring growth of grass.

The couple of dozen sheep and their lambs gave my parents some wool to sell and lambs to take to market when they were grown to the right size.

Fairly early in their lives, all lambs had to have their long tails bobbed — cut off short. The male lambs suffered the added trauma of having their testicles removed.

We children felt it was awfully cruel but my father assured us that it didn't hurt the lambs very much, and was a job that someone had to do. We could readily see that all sorts of burrs and stickers had collected in the wool on a lamb's tail. Manure also clung to the wool and added to the messy problem. So, the tails had to come off, leaving a two-inch stub!

Nothing could keep us from watching, as each tail was "bobbed." Some pine-tar ointment was immediately applied to the bleeding stub to prevent infection, and off each lamb went bouncing away to join the other sheep.

Can you imagine a family then eating those lambs' tails? My father told us we just couldn't imagine how good they would taste if we would only try them. We listened but didn't believe that such a messy bunch of things could be eaten.

My father skinned each tail carefully, washed them and delivered them to my mother for cooking. Although my memory isn't clear as to how she prepared the lamb tails, it is totally clear in how delicious they were! I just couldn't imagine anything tasting any better.

* * * * *

I didn't like our pigs as much as the sheep. Their pen smelled so bad! I also was afraid of them. Our parents warned us children against getting into the pig pen. Roy and I knew what they were saying when we would sit on the top timber of the pen and watch an unwary chicken get a little too close and become an immediate dinner for one of our pigs.

One time a neighbor gave us a tiny pig that weighed less than five pounds. It wouldn't have lasted a minute in the pen with the grown pigs, so a little house was built for it, and the baby pig was given the run of our yard. The little thing took a bottle even more readily than a lamb. It was messy and always hungry but became a pet and an increasing nuisance. When it reached 50 pounds, the pig approached anyone entering the yard, nuzzled their legs and grunted for a handout. Needless to say the pig thrived on choice scraps from the table and an endless supply of acorns from the oak trees and pepperwood tree close by.

It wasn't long before the little five-pound pig was a 200-pound hog, now very forceful in insisting on getting food. You hardly dared go outside. He shoved us around so energetically that my mother finally insisted that the animal be sold. None of us children resisted. We had become fearful that our "pet" would eat us if we didn't immediately meet the hog's food demands.

Once or twice each year a pig was butchered for home use rather than being sold. It was a great event for us and our grandparents. Once the big animal was hit in the head with a sledge hammer, and it's throat slit so all of the blood would drain out, it was dumped into a huge container of boiling water.

After only a minute or two in the scalding water, the hog was hoisted out and laid on a big table under the trees. Razor-sharp knives were used to scrape off the dense hog bristles (hair). The hog's skin was pink! It was a beautiful sight.

The hog was immediately butchered and cut into pieces of meat ready for eating. The "hams" were set aside for smoking. Fresh pork was something we didn't often have and was enjoyed by all of us. I do remember the constant warning about making sure the pork was thoroughly cooked. No attempt was made to make bacon. My father really enjoyed chewing on the rind that came with certain pieces of pork.

One of the things I liked best about hog-raising was watching my father prepare cooked whole wheat for part of the animals' winter feed. The same huge cooking pot used to scald a hog in preparation for removing bristles was now used to cook wheat. More than 200 pounds of wheat was cooked at one time. The big iron pot was hung from a steel scaffold positioned over a fire pit. Several hours and regular stirring were needed to cook the wheat.

I loved the smell of the steaming wheat and taking spoonfuls out of the pot to eat. I've never lost the taste for whole grain cooked wheat and it's a smell I still remember.

My father did his best to keep abreast of techniques of growing a good wheat crop. He had read about nitrogen-fixing crops, and regularly planted many acres to vetch.

He would not only harvest and sell part of the vetch seed, but would follow that crop with wheat to gain the extra nitrogen from the vetch.

He would treat the seed for new vetch plantings with a coating of mud from established areas. My brother and I had the horrible job of taking a bucket and shovel and bringing back dirt from a quarter-mile away. We had to carry the 50-60 pound bucket of dirt by sharing the weight through use of the shovel handle.

One serious problem eventually ended the wheat growing. The torrents of winter rains, often totaling one hundred inches and more, tore through the top layer of plowed soil. Ditches three feet wide and two feet deep were dug as the avalanche of water made its way to the Mattole River. Hundreds of tons of my father's best topsoil ended up in the river. With most of the "grain" land on a gentle slope, there was no way to correct the situation except to allow natural grasses to re-establish themselves and hold more of the soil in place.

* * * * *

Our two or three cows were a really important part of mountain family living. Careful planning resulted in our cows having their calves in February or early March of each year. The prior October or November the cows were "dried up" so they had a good rest before calving. It resulted in lots of milk during the spring and summer.

The calves were allowed to nurse for a few weeks and then fed artificial milk substitute until they could eat grass, hay and grain.

The cows were allowed to roam free most of the year and were milked once each day, in early evening. By the time I was six and Roy seven and a half, the milking became our job for the most part. After school and before dinner we would find the cows and milk them. Most times they would be at the barn where straw and occasional grain was available for them.

I don't know what convinced the cows to stand still for two little boys to milk them, but for some reason they usually did.

Now and then Roy and I couldn't locate the cows on this big ranch and we would return to the house with empty pails. My father always had a way of calling and locating the animals and between everyone, we got the day's milk home, though sometimes in the darkness.

Milk was handled in one of two ways. Sometimes it was allowed to sit in pans overnight. The cream that had risen to the top was skimmed off and used fresh or for making butter. The skim milk became hog feed if not used for making fresh cottage cheese.

Sometimes the whole milk was put through a cream separator while still warm. The separator was a magnificent machine with a huge iron frame and stainless steel discs to separate the cream from the milk. The separator was bolted to the floor of our pantry.

Roy's and my job was to turn the crank on the separator faster and faster until a bell began to ring with each turn. That signaled that the unit containing the scores of stainless steel discs was now whirling at the desired speed. I'm not certain but it likely was turning at several thousand rpm's.

At that point the spigot was turned on and milk allowed to flow into the center of the disc assembly. A marvelous thing happened. Out of one spout came pure cream; out of the other came skim milk.

Cream was what we were after. It was then poured into special 2-gallon cans and shipped to a creamery about sixty miles away. Our mailman would haul the full can of cream to it's destination as he made his route and return an empty can. No doubt my father paid the mailman for doing this. It may have been a regular postal service offered to anyone. Most of the skim milk continued to help feed our growing family of pigs.

As fall arrived and the cows produced less milk the small shipments to the creamery were halted. Cream was accumulated to make butter for winter use. Churning cream into butter wasn't an easy job. It was mostly done by my mother. The butter churn handle took endless turning at a pretty constant rate before, suddenly, the cream turned into chunks of butter. Roy and I helped sometimes by taking turns with turning the handle of the churn.

When the butter formed it was separated from the remaining liquid and packaged for daily use or stored in big crocks for winter use. A certain amount of salt was first worked into the new butter. Although I don't remember clearly, a heavy salt solution was likely poured over the crock of butter before the lid was put on.

The stored butter tasted just a little bit stale after several months in the crock, but was always welcome and a wonderful taste to go with hot, homemade bread that was so much a part of most meals.

Quite often we children had bread and milk as a main supper dish. I remember it tasting awfully good, chunks of homemade bread, covered with milk, and with some sugar on top.

Unlike normal dairy operations, our several cows were "dried up" at the same time, usually in October, and not milked again until March. Sometimes during the winter they would give birth to their calves. We would begin taking the milk from the cows when the calves were a month or two old.

"Drying up" a cow meant that we took only part of the milk from a cow each evening. Within a couple of weeks the animal's system produced less and less milk, and then none at all.

I didn't ask my parents why we didn't "dry up" one cow at a time so we could enjoy fresh milk all winter. Later on I realized that our animals had very little winter feed. Without an abundance of green grass their feed was mainly the straw from our summer grain harvest. It wouldn't have had enough nutrients to allow production of milk.

Once our milk cows were dried up for the winter, condensed milk became part of our regular diet for several months. To me, "canned" milk tasted fine, though different from fresh milk. Trips my father made during the winter to buy supplies resulted in his bringing home several 24 or 48-can cartons of "Carnation" or "Pet" canned milk. When the huge cartons of things like shredded wheat or corn flakes were emptied we made wonderful inside-the-house playhouses of them.

Corn flakes and shredded wheat became a major part of our breakfast diet for most of the winter months. I'm sure there were fried potatoes available regularly as my father felt that potatoes needed to be part of both breakfast and dinner. Potatoes were cheap when bought in 100-lb. bags, and stored well. There was no money for things like ham or bacon but no one complained.

I don't remember any of us ever tiring of eating shredded wheat or corn flakes.

* * * * *

Shearing the sheep was a major activity during several spring days. Wool didn't bring in a lot of money but there was a market for it and any source of income was welcomed by our parents. Shearing each sheep required an hour or more using a device quite like a normal hair clipper. Because there was no electricity in the Mattole Valley, power to activate the shearing clippers had to be produced by hand-turning a special motor. The motor stood atop a tripod about three feet tall. An endless cord connected the motor to the shears, quite like a dentist's drill during the same period of time.

For the several days it took to shear our twenty to thirty sheep, my brother and I alternated in turning the handle that eventually made the clippers work through a series of pulleys and the endless cord. We had to turn the handle at a constant speed for the clippers to cut the wood cleanly. If you slowed down or stopped, the clippers ceased to work and everything came to a standstill.

My father would lay a sheep on it's back on a big piece of canvas and the shearing would begin. One of my father's knees held the animal down. Whichever one of us boys wasn't turning the handle to make the motor go would help hold the sheep's front legs and head. My father always began at the sheep's belly and slowly worked the clippers under the heavy wool, being careful not to nick the animal's skin.

It must have taken most of an hour to shear each sheep, because the neck, head and legs took extra time. The sheep didn't like being caught and treated this way and would occasionally squirm and try to get free. One time a sheep kicked it's back foot so hard in trying to escape that the shears were broken and knocked out of my father's hand. The sharp corner broke off and hit me in the forehead, leaving a big gash and lots of bleeding.

My mother was frantic because we couldn't locate the small broken-off piece of the shears. Her and my father's greatest fear was that it was stuck deep in my head. Shearing was stopped for the time but went on normally within an hour as soon as the last piece of metal was found and a patch put on my head. Turning that handle for hours on end was one of the toughest jobs I can remember on that ranch.

Pretty soon the week-long job was completed, the wool bundled up and delivered to wherever my father took it for sale, and our couple dozen sheep ran around looking very skinny and undressed.

My brother's and my arm muscles soon quit aching. We felt great about helping finish a tough job. The words "self-esteem" may not have become popular yet, but we had lots of it.

Learning About Adults

My older brother, Roy, and I were so close and so constantly together, that few early memories remain of my two younger brothers, or my sister, during the period when I was between five and eight or nine years old. Roy likely looked upon me as a pest at times. I never wanted to let him out of my sight and forever wanted to be part of what he did.

One event, and not a happy one, stands out yet. My father had taken my pregnant mother to a hospital about fifty miles away for the birth of my youngest brother.

Our grandmother, my father's mother, was living in our house while our parents were away. For some reason I wet my bed during the night. I was ashamed and terrified and my grandmother was furious. She tried to grab me to give me a spanking but I ran out of the house and crawled under it, way back in the dirt so she couldn't reach me. My grandmother was a fairly large, stout woman and there was no way she could crawl after me. I must have stayed there for over an hour. She finally agreed not to punish me if I would come out.

Our grandmother was really a very kind and thoughtful person. Each year Roy and I helped her crack walnuts harvested from a big tree near their prior home up on a mountain several miles away. We would work two or three hours at a time shelling the big bags of walnuts. Some of these my grandparents kept for baking and stuff. Most were taken to a market in a big town and sold.

The big question in our minds was, "How much is Grandma going to pay us?" No one dared bring up the subject. We chatted about everything else, but you can be sure it was pretty often on our minds, at least mine.

At the end of each nut-cracking session, our grandmother would tell us, "You boys wait right here for just a minute and I'll have something for you." It was always fifteen or twenty cents which we considered a huge amount of money.

As I remember, the only other way Roy and I had to make some money was to sweep the leaves and needles off the roofs of the cabins in our grandparents' campground. Grandpa, with his bad leg, couldn't climb safely up on the roofs, so he would divide up the job and let my brother and me sweep the roofs clean. It always took about half an hour for each roof. We felt completely safe in our bare feet even on the slanted roofs. The pay was always five cents for each roof.

Every time we walked over to our grandparents' campground, you can be sure our eyes went to the cabin roofs, hoping to see a bunch of debris that needed removal.

* * * * *

Our way to school led us down into a canyon, across a bridge covering the creek, then up the other side of the canyon to where the dirt road leveled off again. As we walked up the grade out of the canyon, we always peeked carefully to see if a neighbor's big bull might be standing near the pasture fence next to the road.

The bull's presence really frightened my brother and me. It seemed to us that the bull towered above the barbed-wire fence, and could walk over it or push through it at will. We wouldn't go a step further, but walked the half mile back home. My mother always insisted that my father walk back with us. He tried to tell us we shouldn't be afraid as the bull was on the other side of the fence, but we weren't at all convinced. When we reached the top of the canyon, my father would run shouting towards the bull, throwing some rocks at the same time. The bull always trotted away and we proceeded on to school, but we never gained the courage to take that bull on by ourselves.

We tried to be brave, but what if that huge bull saw us as little people and charged through the fence to gore us?

* * * * *

In some ways salesmen coming through the Mattole River Valley were welcomed by my parents. They always saved some purchases for the Raleigh Products or Watkins Products representatives. We children would gather outside while they showed our parents their well-stocked vans. Items such as vanilla extract, ground pepper and chocolate were frequently bought that way. It was a way, too, of finding out more about the outside world, especially once the same salesman came by several times in a row, and the man became sort of a "friend."

One time a salesman selling heavy aluminum cookware arrived at our house. My parents listened to the middle-aged, well-dressed professional salesman for more than an hour, while he extolled the health and taste benefits of "waterless cooking" in his beautiful but expensive pots and pans.

It turned out that families who were interested were all to be invited to a big dinner at a well-known neighbor's home several miles away. It was to be a Saturday night and children were welcome. The salesman said he wanted us to experience first-hand the advantages he was claiming. The dinner was free with no obligation to buy anything!

We children were most excited. Except for an occasional meal with our grandparents, we just didn't go out to dinner, ever! My father had mentioned occasionally about having gone out to dinner and eaten a big Porterhouse steak as part of a several course dinner. That had been difficult to picture, but here we were going to be part of something like that.

I remember that dinner as being sort of okay, but it wasn't nearly as good as eating at home. My biggest disappointment was the potatoes. They had been steamed and served with the peels on, and with some butter if we wanted it. To me it was blah.

Potatoes at home were almost always mashed with butter and milk, and served with the best-tasting gravy you could imagine. Chicken or other meats were usually pan-fried and always resulted in the makings of the tasty gravy.

I waited and waited for dessert to finally arrive. It was a baked or steamed apple with whipped cream on the top. It was only "pretty good" at best. My mother's whipped cream was flavored with vanilla and a little sugar. If allowed, you could practically eat an entire bowl of it! This whipped cream was just that, cream that was whipped. It didn't taste nearly like whipped cream should. I could overhear the adults raving about everything!

My parents did buy a bunch of the cookware, probably more than they could afford. I don't recall how many changes in my mother's cooking methods resulted from the purchases, but that salesman was most skilled and convincing.

* * * * *

Before we left our mountain ranch our parents told us we were going to have a visitor from Virginia. My mother did her best to explain to those of us who asked questions, why she could have two fathers, one living in Lodi and this one coming three-thousand miles from the East Coast.

She explained that her real mother had died suddenly from an illness leaving her three older sisters and herself, then about two years old. Her father felt he could handle raising the three older girls but not a two-year old. A close friend's family asked if they could adopt my mother into their family.

My mother later told me that it was an unofficial adoption, just an agreement and a handshake. My mother's adopting father apparently asked only for absolute assurance that her real father "would never, under any circumstances, ask for the child's return."

This visit was the first time my mother was to see her real father since she was two, and of course she had no memory at all of him. His name was Robert Leathco and she referred to him as "Pop Bob." I know she was excited and nervous at the same time.

The visit went well as I remember. I know my mother took a lot of pride in showing off her little family. I'm sure "Pop Bob" was amazed to find his little girl living way up in the mountains and so effectively mothering four or five little ones. I do know there were tears at the parting as both probably knew, despite assurances otherwise, that they would never again see each other.

This turned out to be true. When I was 12-13, living on our first Lodi dairy, I recall my father encouraging my mother to take the trip to Virginia to see Pop Bob and her sisters. At times the discussion ended in a serious argument.

My mother was caught in the middle of a situation where she desperately wanted to see her "other family" but where she valued her children's welfare more.

In the end my mother always turned down the suggestion emphatically. My brothers and I encouraged her to make the two-week trip, but inside, I'm not sure we wanted to be alone with a very stern father with a bad temper.

* * * * *

With all of the ranch-produced grain plus lots of open feeding areas, raising turkeys was something our parents decided to try. The prospects looked good for selling fine turkeys in the holiday market. It all began with the purchase of baby turkeys. The wheat we raised brought so little money selling it directly that my father held enough of it back for the flock of turkeys, to be used once they could handle the whole grain.

Because there were no electric wires yet strung through the Mattole Valley, the little turkeys were kept warm at night under the big, metal hoods, with straw for bedding. Kerosene was used to fuel the portable heaters under the hoods. It was the same fuel used in the wick lamps used to provide lighting in the house.

One night we were awakened by my mother screaming. The turkey house was on fire and going up in flames reaching twenty feet high. My father raced outside but nothing could be done. All of his 200 partly-grown turkeys, the shed and equipment were gone, along with his dreams of some added income.

I guess we were fortunate there wasn't a north wind or our house, about fifty feet away, would have been burned to the ground. The couple of hoses mainly used to irrigate our small garden, provide water for the dozen fruit trees, and give us a source of water for the chickens, could do nothing against this big fire.

* * * * *

Another project that could have helped our family's harsh financial situation was a two-acre patch of potatoes put in one spring in an especially fertile corner of the ranch about a quarter-mile from our house, just off the road taking us to school.

My father put a lot of time into plowing, harrowing and readying the field for planting. He showed us how the "eyes" in the purchased seed potatoes determined how the potato would be cut into sections for placement several inches deep in the ground. We had seen a few potato plants in our garden and realized that one plant could provide as many as a dozen good potatoes. My father told us he had old grain bags all ready to be filled with the harvested potatoes. We couldn't help but be excited as we watched those potato vines grow beautifully over the next several months. Occasionally my father would dig down and show us potatoes getting almost ready for harvest.

Early one evening my father yelled, "Come on!," unsnapped our dog Coaly (all black, of course) and went running down the road towards his almost-mature potato patch. Apparently he had heard the familiar sound of grunting hogs in that quiet evening and the sounds came from the direction of his potato patch.

Our dog was never allowed to run loose. Coaly chased everything, chickens, calves, sheep, pigs, and just couldn't be contained. His leash was attached to a fifty-foot wire stretched between two big trees. It allowed him lots of exercise and shade during the summers.

When my brother and I arrived at the potato patch, Coaly was nipping at the hogs who were running in all directions in an attempt to escape. The woman neighbor who owned the hogs was screaming at my father, "Call your dog off my pigs!" My father was shouting back "Get your d—- pigs out of my potatoes!" The angry woman picked up a big clod of dirt and threw it at my father, hitting him. My father's response was pretty mild for a man with his bad temper, "If you weren't a woman, I'd knock you down."

The potato crop was a near disaster. Apparently the hogs had discovered the potatoes several days earlier and had been rooting out and feasting on the almost-grown crop.

I felt so badly for my father. He deserved a lot better and must have felt awfully discouraged and helpless as he looked at his devastated field.

* * * * *

I imagine that children of every family who celebrate Christmas would believe in Santa Claus forever if it were their choice.

There were very few gifts under our undecorated fir tree at Christmas, but always something for everyone. We used our own real sox for "stockings" which regularly contained an orange and banana and even exotic things like Brazil nuts. We children "believed" totally.

This one morning, several days after Christmas, our school mate, Leland, crossed his family's pasture and joined us for the balance of the walk to school. The conversation had to turn immediately to Christmas and what things we received. It wasn't long before Leland challenged us with, "Do you know that your mom and dad are Santa Claus?"

Roy and I were stunned! We gave him a dozen reasons, and "proof" of why there had to be a real Santa Claus. But Leland was relentless. He suggested we ask our parents. We did just that the minute we got home after school, and were forced to grow up one more notch that winter day.

Only once during our seven years living in our house in the Mattole River Valley did we travel away for Christmas. We went to Lodi to spend this holiday with our other grandparents, my mother's parents.

It was a long ride in our small Chevrolet sedan, almost 300 miles. It must have been torture for our parents to handle and feed five children on a continuous ride that surely must have taken ten or twelve hours. Somehow, I remember little about the trip. On any drives of over a few hours, we always had lots of crackers and cheese, and juicy things like apples. No stops were made except for gasoline or bathroom needs! I do have vivid memories of two things once we arrived at our grandparents' home. These were the sounds of trains passing through Lodi at night, and the gifts for Christmas.

My grandfather told us what each sequence of "toots" by the train engineer meant. I just loved those sounds. It sort of reassured me that everything was right with the world. The tracks were only two blocks away and ran parallel to the street where my grandparents lived. We slept on the second floor and could hear every sound made by the rail cars rolling on the tracks through Lodi. I would always hope there might be just one more train before I fell asleep.

Everything else seemed like nothing when we saw our "main" Christmas presents. Our grandparents had purchased scooters for Roy and me and tricycles for each of our younger brothers and for our sister, the youngest child.

Our scooters had wheels with roller bearings and were almost soundless as we whizzed up and down the concrete sidewalk in front of our grandparents' house.

Perhaps I should add another wonderful memory. It was the smell of toast being made each morning by our grandmother. In "big" towns like Lodi sliced bread was regularly available. Our grandmother, though, liked to make toast with "unsliced" bread. That way she could cut thicker slices. Most mornings she would ask one of us to run down to the little bakery only a few blocks away, and buy a loaf of unsliced bread.

Christmas had to end and all seven of us jammed back into the little Chevy touring car and headed for home.

All of the tricycles and scooters had to be roped onto the back of the car.

Everything arrived intact at our ranch house except my scooter. The two lovely varnished wooden handles with the long bolt through the center, had chattered loose during the trip and were forever lost.

I know I cried when I realized what had happened. My father was a good mechanic and did his best to put together make-shift handles. Nothing, however, worked very well. The handles just couldn't be duplicated with the tools and materials my father had available.

My parents allowed all of us to ride our scooters on the gravel-covered dirt road running in front of our house. That was okay, but didn't work too well because of the gravel throwing the wheels off balance. There was no way to get up any speed, but it was fun.

In winter we were allowed to race the scooters up and down the long living room. That surely must have kept our parents' nerves on edge, but the wooden plank floors didn't seem to suffer.

* * * * *

Although we lived fifty miles from the nearest big town, boys still needed to have haircuts. My father did this as needed for us four boys. Someone looking at old family pictures commented that my father must have placed bowls over each boy's head and cut off any hair that stuck out.

Somehow, though, my father gained a reputation of an accomplished barber. The poorer families occasionally brought a boy over for a haircut. No charge was ever made.

One mother brought her boy, Leland, over to our house for a haircut. His family usually took him elsewhere, like to a town barber. I couldn't understand why he cried during much of the haircutting. I realized that those hand clippers sometimes pulled hairs, but wondered about the tears. Leland's mother was embarrassed. My father was angry, though tried not to show it. That wasn't a haircut he offered to do again.

My father continued to give haircuts to all family members, including my sister, until I was well into high school. At that point he began giving Roy and me the fifty cents for a professional haircut.

* * * * *

Parties of any nature were few and far between for our family. It wasn't something we thought much about and surely didn't miss. The greatest excitement of an entire summer came when our parents were invited to a housewarming for a neighbor who had built a new home about a quarter-mile from us. It was up a hill and out of sight of the main road. We knew building was underway, but we children weren't permitted to go near the site. Besides, we just didn't stray far from home except to explore parts of our ranch.

Children were invited to the party! It probably wasn't so much that the hosts wanted a bunch of children, but that children most often had to be where their parents were. If there were such things as "baby-sitters," I had never heard of one.

There was noise, excitement, a live band, and likely plenty of alcohol in addition to soft drinks and cider.

What an evening for a seven-year-old who had never seen dozens of people together in a party atmosphere!

People began to pair up and dance. I had never seen that done, either. My father and mother didn't drink at all. If our single alcoholic neighbor came down the road and hesitated near our gate, we all hid in a back room and never answered the knock if that occurred. My father ridiculed people who drank alcohol.

I don't believe my father knew how to dance. He was there to enjoy the visiting, the food and the conviviality.

I'm not certain about my mother's dancing ability. She was a city girl and a beautiful young woman. Her father had been the mayor of Lodi. She finally accepted one of what had to be many requests for a dance.

It wasn't five minutes later that my father announced that we were leaving…now! My father was jealous and apparently absolutely could not stand the idea of his wife being held by another man, even during a dance.

Bits of the discussion reached our young ears as we drove home. My mother insisted, as gently as she could, that there was no harm done. She wanted to be a little part of this special party. My father, though, was heading for home, determined and angry. If any other party invitations came our way, I was never aware of them.

* * * * *

It was late spring! We couldn't believe it when our teacher announced that our little school had been selected as the site for an area-wide track meet. Five schools were to compete. There were to be all sorts of short races, plus high jumps, broad jumps, baseball throws and relays.

Our teacher immediately laid out areas for practice running and jumping. She even set up a couple of posts with a bamboo crossbar for practicing high jumping. It was sort of scary to most of us. We had never done anything like this before.

It was a big day. Parents and teachers had arrived early that Saturday to set up running and jumping areas. White chalk lines were everywhere. Our parents and younger brothers came to watch and encourage us. My next younger brother was in the first grade. He would be competing. Events were scheduled by grades. I knew I would be competing against my older brother, Roy.

I'll always remember the drive home afterwards. Roy had won a blue, red and white ribbon. I was so proud of him. He had run and jumped with the best at our class level.

Even my first grade brother, Don, had a ribbon to show.

I remember trying to justify my coming away empty-handed by suggesting the races should have been run by age, not grade level. My parents tried to console me, but it was a long ride home.

* * * * *

The final winter we lived on our big ranch my father told us that we were going into the Christmas tree business. When he had driven to Eureka the previous holiday season for supplies, my father said he noticed lots of people paying a dollar or two for fir Christmas trees.

His idea was to select and cut three hundred beautiful fir trees to sell in the big town of Eureka, about sixty miles away.

It wasn't difficult to locate trees to cut. There were thousands growing on the hills and flat areas of our ranch. We worked much of the time in the rain, cutting down perfectly-shaped trees ranging from four to ten feet tall. It was a three or four day job, cutting the trees and then carrying or dragging them to the truck where my father packed them tightly together.

Although it was very hard and cold work it was made exciting because we could talk and dream about all of the money to be made. Not only would there be extra things for Christmas, but also to help buy needed things for the year ahead. My father wondered aloud as to why he hadn't thought of doing this in earlier years. My older brother and I were good at arithmetic and it took very little time to figure out how much money would come from three hundred trees sold at one dollar apiece or even seventy-five or fifty cents. My father assured all of us that he had seen dozens of people paying these prices at Christmas tree lots in Eureka when he had been there the year before.

My father told us that if we stuck with the job all of the way until the truck was loaded, that he would share some of the money with us. We had visions of even a dollar or two each. He didn't need to say much more. It became less effort to drag even the heavy trees to the truck.

One serious accident, when the tree-cutting work was almost finished, took a lot of our high spirits away. My next younger brother, Don, about six at the time, wanted to be part of the effort and helped where he could. My father wasn't nearby when the injury happened. We had cut part way through a tree and then bent it over to finish cutting. Roy was using a full-sized double-bitted ax. Don and I were holding the tree down in position for the cut. Roy's ax bounced off the tree and the sharp blade hit Don in the mouth, leaving a tooth half cut off and a lip cut through to the bone.

All of us ran to the house as fast as we could, trying to tell Don that he was going to be okay. I remember my mother screaming at the sight of Don's injury.

Without doctors available, parents in these out-of-the-way communities did the best they could in emergencies. The bleeding finally stopped, some iodine was applied and Don suffered through the situation until healing took place. The tooth wasn't replaced at the time and a scar remains to this day.

Cutting and loading Christmas trees had to continue without Don and the hour came when the truck was packed high with fresh fir trees, and roped down for the long drive to Eureka. No one accompanied my father. He took several blankets so he could sleep in his truck and save money.

Three days later my father arrived home, exhausted and defeated. No one would buy a single tree. After two days he drove his truck to the Salvation Army building and gave them all of his trees. It was a sad homecoming for all of us.

Looking back, this Christmas tree fiasco probably indicated the dire state of the economy in 1929. It certainly must have told our parents that they had lost the fight to keep their ranch. They just had no money left to make the ranch payments after providing for the family's minimum needs.

Though he would of course never admit it, my father must have realized that "living off the land" was not nearly as romantic as he hoped it would be at the time he first homesteaded his 40 acres when he was 23-24.

Learning About Adults 61

He had taken care of his growing family with determination. We never lacked for something to eat. He had never asked for charity from someone else. But he couldn't make the ranch payments and reality had to be faced.

Our Family Moves To Town

Early the next summer my father announced that we were moving to the town of Lodi. We, as children, really didn't know what was behind the change. We felt good where we were. School was rewarding and usually fun. If we were poor, we weren't aware of it. There was always something to eat, though often it was the same as the day before.

One day my father told us three boys that we needed to tell our teacher we were to check out of school because we were moving.

We were both excited and sad. My mother didn't want us to leave school just yet, but my father insisted, so we checked out. From experience my mother knew well that my father usually underestimated the time required to do a job. He was always overly optimistic. She saw no reason for us to be hanging around the ranch when school was in session and we could be going along with our studies.

The reality of the time required to prepare for moving from a big farm slowly became apparent. Three weeks later only half of the stuff was sorted and packed or discarded. There was little we children could do. When cars passed by the ranch we kept out of sight. It was embarrassing to still be there when we had told all of our school friends that we were moving "in a few days."

Six weeks passed before my father climbed into our 1½ ton Chevy truck, stacked high beyond belief with family belongings and small farm items, and drove away for the 300-mile drive to Lodi. His plan was to leave the loaded truck parked at our other grandparents' (my mother's parents) home and then take a bus or other transportation back to our ranch.

There were probably flat tires and engine problems, but my father always figured out how to get things repaired and he arrived back home on schedule.

Shortly after his return and saying a final good-bye to our paternal grandparents, all of us were loaded into the family car. With cheese, crackers, apples and milk to snack on we made the final leg of the move to Lodi.

My mother wasn't fighting the move at all. She had gone along willingly with my father's dream of becoming a mountain rancher and enjoying the freedom of being his own boss. She had seen him willingly give up his promising job as a bank teller in Lodi just for the chance to be on his own.

My mother was part of a closely-knit family and had only seen her parents two or three times in about ten years. It would mean, too, that she wouldn't have to endure the fear of injuries or sickness in her growing family without available medical help. She would gladly leave the horrors of the frequent earthquakes behind. I am certain, though she never said so, that she welcomed the move out of those mountains.

I'm equally sure my father felt only failure. He had lost his ranch after seven years of hard work.

Our Family Moves To Town

* * * * *

For a short period our entire family lived with my mother's parents in their big two-story home in Lodi. It was school summer vacation there, so the selection of schools wasn't a question until a house was located to rent.

I remember well the small white house with a big front porch and a porch-rail you could sit on. It was in a rather poor part of town but a large enough house to hold us and no doubt all my parents could afford. I know my mother was pleased with the little house and its clean kitchen. As the winter came on, it was wonderful to have a house that kept the wind and rain outside. No buckets were now needed to catch drops of water from the ceiling.

It didn't take my father long to dislike the family living in the house to one side of us. They had a German name and the parents had a slight accent. It turned out that this family had fairly recently moved to Lodi from North Dakota. My father had spent some Navy time in World War I and the enemy were Germans. Now anything "German" seemed to be still an enemy to him and was suspected of misdeeds.

This suspicion really showed when all of our chickens housed in the little shed next to the alley were stolen one night. My father had every reason to be dismayed. Here he had caged those birds carefully and trucked them all of those 300 miles to Lodi. They were to be the source of fresh eggs for his family. Those chickens were one of the few ties my father had with his beloved big ranch that no longer was his.

We felt badly too, and even more so when my father was outspoken in blaming our German neighbor for the theft of his chickens. My mother had to plead with him to prevent an open confrontation with this neighbor.

* * * * *

Our sister wasn't yet old enough for school but all four boys were enrolled at close-by schools when the fall semester began. My older brother and I were in the fourth grade.

I never felt really good about my new school. It seemed I seldom understood how to do the work as quickly as the other students. Taking tests was especially difficult as they seemed so different from the more casual ones given by the young teacher in our one-room Upper Mattole School, where there were only four students in our grade.

We walked the half-dozen blocks home for lunch each day. If my mother or father hadn't had a chance to go to the store, we sometimes had to then run down for a quart of milk or a box of shredded wheat or corn flakes. The ads for Nabisco Shredded Wheat at the time always rang through my head, "Twelve biscuits for twelve cents."

I liked our neighbors' children. It turned out that most were girls and they were very friendly. One afternoon on the way home from school alone, a tough neighborhood boy decided he was going to beat up on me. I was terrified! As he started trotting across the street after me, a girl seemed to come streaking from nowhere and drove the boy away. It was one of our neighbor girls who was in the sixth grade. She had saved my life and I had another good reason to like our neighbors, even though my father had told us not to associate with them.

* * * * *

Through the summer and fall my father took odd jobs to buy food and pay the rent. He was determined to not have his family on "charity."

Only one job do I remember at all, and that is because my brother and I were part of it on weekends during the first winter. The job consisted of gathering up and burning prunings from grapevines. Once the vines became dormant following grape harvest, pruners came in and cut back all of the prior seasons new growth, leaving just three to five-inch stubs. The cut-off vine parts, up to six feet long, were left on the ground where they dropped! Someone had to rake or carry the cuttings to a central area where they were burned. The vineyard owner paid one cent per vine to have this done.

During weekdays my father worked at this job alone. It was cold and wet work but by starting early he could clean an area of 300-400 vines and earn $3-$4. On weekends the three of us could increase a day's earnings to $5-$6. The vineyard owner was a very religious man and preferred that we didn't work on Sundays. The five or six dollars meant too much to our family, however, and the owner "looked the other way" when we were in his vineyards on Sundays.

My mother would fix up a quart thermos of hot chocolate, and made enough sandwiches to keep us going. Especially on days when it was raining lightly or when the fog was thick we could hardly wait for the morning "break" and for lunch. I will always remember that wonderful hot chocolate. We would sit on old boxes or stand by the fire from the burning grape limbs and talk about how many vines we had done so far and set sort of a goal for the day. It wasn't long each day before our pants legs and shoes got soaked, but sitting or standing by the fire sipping hot chocolate seemed to make everything okay. Keeping two eight- to ten-year-old boys enthused when their hands and feet were cold was never easy, but my father did his best by occasionally announcing the progress we were making.

If my father had other odd jobs during the several months we lived on Hilborn Street, I have no memory of them.

The employment situation was very harsh. People who had jobs hung on to them. As a farmer my father didn't have many skills that were needed in towns.

I'm sure my mother's parents must have helped out where they could, without bringing on the ire of my father.

* * * * *

Sometime during the first winter our parents were able to rent a small house with a couple of acres of ground a few miles out of town. Here we could have a big garden and, as it turned out, two milk goats. My father wanted a milk cow, but couldn't spare the money to buy one.

The move to our little house in the country meant enrolling in another school to complete the fourth grade. I remember immediately liking that school and the teacher. Her name was Mrs. Battalana. Some of the older boys called her "Mrs. Battle-ax" when she couldn't hear them, but I thought she was a pretty wonderful person.

My brothers and I walked home each day for lunch, which usually consisted of a bowl of cold cereal and milk. School was less than a half mile away and walking home for lunch wasn't a problem.

The problem was the milk! It came from the two goats my father had bought. Each evening, Roy and I milked the goats. They were kind of easy to milk because they were small and friendly animals. On the other hand, their teats weren't shaped like cows' and you couldn't get the same kind of grip. My father always tethered them out to feed on grass during the day. At night they were fed hay and grain and put into a little shed to keep them safe from roaming dogs. There was no fence around the property.

Goat's milk tasted very different from the cow's milk we were accustomed to. No matter what my father said or did, or tried to show us by example how good it tasted, we disliked the goat's milk. Even when poured over shredded wheat or corn flakes, with sugar, the milk was a strange taste to us. There was no alternate so we tried to get used to goat's milk, but used it as sparingly as possible.

Roy and I completed our fourth grade at Henderson School and did well in our classes. The one event that stands out happened late one morning. Our teacher called my brother and me into a separate room and told us she had a secret we must keep. We walked out of that room certain that we were the most important people in the entire world.

Mrs. Battalana told us we mustn't tell another student, but rush home for an early lunch. When we returned a bus would be waiting to take the entire class to watch a big dirigible land at a nearby airport. I couldn't believe how lucky we were and how important I felt to have this information our teacher had shared with no one else. It was exciting as we had never seen a dirigible before. It was fascinating to watch the crew pull and hold the airship down with long ropes.

During some afternoons after school I remember seeing my father and mother sitting in our sedan. He was reading serial stories to her that appeared regularly in the daily newspaper. I thought that was nice.

We Become Dairymen

Several weeks after finishing our fourth grade, my father made a deal to become the sharecropper-operator of a Grade B dairy. The milk produced went into producing condensed milk and butter.

We moved during the summer into an old 2-story house on a one-hundred acre ranch located ten miles west of Lodi. Now we had cow's milk to drink, lots of space for chickens, plus good ground and water for a garden.

With the move, though, came the need to milk thirty cows each morning and night. The milk was poured from buckets into ten-gallon cans, then carried 150 feet to the cooling shed, where the cans were placed in water to cool.

Late every morning a big truck arrived. The driver loaded our full ten-gallon cans onto his truck and left us our "empties." All of the cans had numbers painted on them so the creamery could weigh the milk and pay the proper dairy. I always admired the driver's muscles. It couldn't be easy to swing those ninety-pound full cans up four feet to the truck bed.

My brother, Roy, was 11; I was 9½. The cows were ready for milking the same night we moved in. It was a job that must be done, no matter how tired everyone was from moving family belongings to this big ranch.

I can't remember a single thing about that first night's work or that of the following morning. I assume Roy and I milked four or five cows each and that my father milked the balance. I imagine, too, that my mother cared for the three younger children and had dinner ready when the cows were milked, the cattle fed and released for the night, and our first cans of milk placed in the water to cool.

I know my parents had to be both hopeful and apprehensive about their contract to run this dairy. Their contribution was their labor.

The owner, then the District Attorney for San Joaquin County, would provide all the costs of running the dairy operation, including the electricity costs for the home we lived in.

Hopefully, the ranch would produce all of the feed needed for the dairy cattle. If not, the costs were his.

My parents would receive, in payments every two weeks, half of the money received from the sale of all of the milk shipped to the creamery. It was in our interests to get the best milk production from the owner's cows.

My father was excited about our ability to make a good steady income. My mother liked the stability she felt and a decent, though old home for her family.

* * * * *

My 5th, 6th, 7th and 8th grades all were covered in a two-room school located about half of a mile from our ranch. The teacher for those grades was a single woman, Miss Potter, then about fifty-five years old. She boarded and roomed with a farm couple, with no children, who lived almost directly across the road from us. The wife was also a teacher in another very small school.

Each day Miss Potter seemed to drive to school early and came home quite a while after school classes were over. I have no idea what she did on weekends or during summers. She was a very private person.

Miss Potter also was a most effective teacher. She had to be, teaching all four grades and covering all of the subjects from spelling, arithmetic and grammar through history and geography (later to be called social studies, much to my father's displeasure).

The teacher in the adjoining room, Mrs. Mable Benny, taught the four younger grades. She was also the music teacher for students in Miss Potter's room. Our final twenty minutes of most school days was spent in our music lesson with Mrs. Benny. The younger children would have already gone home.

My father immediately liked Miss Potter. She shared his political philosophy; she was also very strict and fair.

I liked Miss Potter. I was an easy student, learned quickly, and thrived on her approval. No one followed directions better than I did. Teachers like those kind of kids. Miss Potter liked me and I tried to live up to her expectations.

It was a whole new classroom situation for Roy and me. Here were thirty to thirty-five students, covering four grades. We entered as fifth graders.

A bench was located near the front of the room, facing the teacher. Miss Potter first called up the fifth graders for arithmetic. We answered questions and received the assignment for the next day.

Next came the sixth graders for their math, followed by the seventh and eighth.

After that came grammar, in the same order. Other subjects had their turn as the morning hours were filled and everyone moved to afternoon subjects following lunch.

During cold or rainy periods we ate lunch in the classroom, and played jackstones by the heater or played hangman on the blackboard.

On pleasant days we older students chose up sides for baseball or played Annie Over.

Miss Potter loved baseball and was usually outside watching the game, and encouraging good plays with a smile.

I found an immense amount of value from listening to the higher grades in their recitations. I got to know in advance what to expect and was always prepared. I guess both Roy and I were "A" students, though Miss Potter used numerical percentage grades, like 70's, 80's or 90's, so I'm not certain.

* * * * *

The rigors and routine of dairy life came to be the normal thing right from the start. Every morning at about 5:00 my brother and I were wakened by our mother. She then stayed up after we left for the milk barn, started the wood fire in the kitchen and made preparations for breakfast and for getting four children off to school.

It was necessary for her to start early as water warmed slowly. Water flowed through a coil of pipes located under the burning wood in the kitchen stove. Without a good fire, you had only cold water. Nothing happened quickly where comfort was concerned.

The first thing my father, Roy and I did on reaching the big barn early each morning was to place alfalfa hay in the mangers in front of the stantions designed to hold the animals' heads in place. Then the big sliding doors opening to the milking area were opened, and we stood back. The cows needed no urging to come into the barn. They crowded and jostled each other to be first in, and quickly poked their heads through the open stantions and began feeding. Our first need was to count twelve cows coming in to each milking area and stop the flow of cows at that point. It was tough to not get run over.

Once the cows had their heads through the stantions, one of us tripped each lock so the animals couldn't withdraw their heads.

Milking cows wasn't an unpleasant job. It was tiring on our hands and wrists for several weeks, but soon Roy and I were able to milk about as many cows as our father. I remember feeling awfully good about being able to fill a pail of milk about as fast as my father or brother.

The warm milk was immediately poured into the ten-gallon cans, and the lids replaced to keep out dust and the ever-present flies.

We may have brought cats with us when we moved to the dairy or they may have just showed up. Either way, cats seemed to be always present, and always producing kittens. Roy and I, and our younger brothers, loved to find the nests of the new kittens. The mother cats never put up a fuss when we held and petted their new families. Often, though, after several days the nest would be empty. It then meant another search to find the new location, often given away by the sound of tiny "meows."

Most of the nests for the kittens would be located on the edge of the big hay storage section of the barn, positioned between the two milking areas.

The cats around the dairy loved nothing more than warm milk. When allowed, they would stand upright on their hind legs in the walking area behind the cows and beg for milk. We would aim a stream of milk from the cow's teat directly at a cat's head. The cats would stand upright until their faces were totally covered by milk froth as they eagerly lapped in the warm milk. My father usually put a stop to this waste of milk though he had a soft spot in his make-up for the dairy cats.

* * * * *

Two areas of the farm quickly became favorites of my older brother and me. One was the big dirt-lined irrigation canal that ran through the 100 acres. The other was our big hay barn.

During winter months the filled hay mow was a great place for any free weekend time. We climbed up on the rafters in the barn and jumped down onto the spongy hay.

Once, after a family trip to a circus, we stretched ropes between rafters in the barn. For hours Roy and I tried to balance ourselves on the ropes, as the circus people had, but with no success whatsoever.

My older brother had no fear of dark, tight spaces. He would spend hours digging tunnels through the tightly-packed hay at the bottom of the stack of alfalfa hay in the barn.

I was very fearful of the tunnels. I did help to pull out the thousands of stems of hay only because I didn't want it known I was scared of the tight tunnels, the darkness and the dust.

The tunnels under the hay got to be long affairs, twenty or thirty feet in length. I had to prove I could make it through them, head down, eyes closed, on hands and knees and so relieved when the other end was reached and I could breathe and see. Although I was part of digging dozens of those "hay tunnels" my fear of them never changed. It was just that I didn't want to be left out of being part of my older brother's activities.

* * * * *

Our pleas to my father to teach us to swim were finally rewarded when he told us one day that first summer to come with him to the bridge over the big irrigation canal. He had a ten foot piece of rope in his hand. It was the only time in the five years we lived on that ranch that my mother walked that quarter mile to the canal. It meant bringing the three smaller children along. She may have had a concern that the flowing water was treacherous. Too, she may have been caught up in our enthusiasm.

No one needed to tell Roy and me that we could learn to swim quickly; we knew that! My father tied the rope in a loop around each of our chests, in turn, and then held the end of the rope as he walked back and forth across the bridge.

My brother and I dog-paddled across the canal a number of times. Before the afternoon was over we had my father remove the loop of rope and we were showing the world we could swim alone. After a few supervised swims, our parents gave us freedom to swim in the big mud-bottomed canal. My mother did it reluctantly but apparently knew we needed the opportunity to gain confidence in the water. My father never swam with us. It just wasn't his way to play games or to be part of his children's activities, other than work or chores.

Fishing in the canal was something we also came to like. The fairly warm water supported the growth of carp, catfish, perch and shiners. The carp had a muddy taste, the perch and shiners were "all bones," but the family enjoyed the few catfish we caught.

Fish poles were always limbs from bushes and trees growing around the ranch. We used ordinary string and tied a single hook on the end. Small metal nuts or washers were tied on for weights. For 10-12 year-olds there wasn't much more exciting as trying to catch fish in the slowly-moving, fairly clear water. Sometimes we caught several dozen little three- to five-inch perch and shiners. After lots of admiring remarks from my mother, the bony fish always went to feed the ever-hungry cats.

When the irrigation season was over, water was cut off at the source, and the canal allowed to drain.

Fish congregated in the deeper areas of the canal. One winter two neighbor boys and we came upon two big salmon stuck in a section of the canal about twenty feet square and two feet deep.

What a bruising fight it was to capture those two fifteen-pound fish! I'm sure we ate them, or tried to, but they had been living in that somewhat muddy water for several weeks.

* * * * *

Getting the barn full of cured alfalfa hay was a summer-long job. The ranch had two fields of alfalfa. One was irrigated with water from a well using a big electric powered pump. The other field of alfalfa was irrigated with water from the irrigation canal we fished and swam in. A number of clover and grass pastures also were irrigated from the canal. Water for the irrigation ditch came from a reservoir, behind a dam on the nearby Mokelumne River.

My brother and I helped with the irrigation when not in school. We could run down to the ends of the long "checks" and report back to our father as to the progress of the water flowing down the checks. He could then adjust or shut off "gates" and open new ones to prevent the small supply ditches from overflowing their banks.

It wasn't always fun for us, because occasionally we worked alone. When water washed around the wooden gates, it was frightening to be alone and find the water out of control. Trying to fill in ditch breaks with man-sized shovels was often not successful, and we had to run for help.

It was much more fun to locate and try to capture pocket gophers during each of the twice monthly alfalfa irrigations. Gophers burrowed underground throughout the alfalfa fields. They thrived on alfalfa roots and killed many plants from their feeding. As water flowed down the checks between low, mounded levees, the gopher holes filled with water. The small animals came out of their burrows or moved to the non-wet part of burrows dug into the higher levee areas. A few shovels of water scooped into the "safe" area usually quickly flushed out the gophers.

We often carried a bucket and took home dead gophers for our cats.

It wasn't kind or fair to the antagonists but occasionally we found a big gopher snake at about the same time we found a drowned-out gopher. We would put them both in the same five-gallon bucket we carried and then marveled at the resulting fight. The gopher always put up a good battle but never won. It bit the snake in a dozen places with it's long teeth, but before long the snake's coils tightened around the gopher's middle and the fight was over.

The snake then always swallowed the gopher whole, starting with the head. Roy and I were totally fascinated with the ability of the snake to stretch it's mouth around a gopher. We remarked about the gopher's tail, as it disappeared, as being the "toothpick" for the snake.

I, especially, liked the snakes living on our ranch. I allowed them to hang around my neck. I felt that garter snakes had a rather bad smell.

* * * * *

During our first year on the dairy farm, my father put together a rabbit hutch. He said he liked rabbit meat and was sure we would. In addition he pointed out that the grasses and alfalfa hay grown on the ranch could provide much of the feed for the rabbits. It would give our family a low-cost meat in addition to our chickens.

I loved the rabbits from the start. They were always friendly, never threatened to bite me, and always seemed to appreciate the grain, hay and fresh water. I didn't handle all of their needs, but did a lot of feeding and watering. It often fell my lot to clean out the wire and lath compartments and remove the accumulation of wet bedding straw and manure. Occasionally the grown rabbits would be seen with drooping ears, almost a sure sign of scab growths inside their ears. To me it was awfully rewarding to watch the rabbits' ears stand up erect again, a few days following application of a few drops of mineral oil.

The female rabbits made marvelous mothers. Before giving birth to a half dozen little, pink, hairless bunnies, they grew a massive mane of hair. You knew that the baby rabbits were about to be born when the mother rabbit had yanked out all of this mane of hair. If you looked into the hutch you would see a beautiful nest lined carefully with all of this mother rabbit's excess hair.

We always waited a week or ten days for the newborn rabbits to grow a little and get some fur before handling them. It was a long wait! Pretty soon all of the little ones, most with white fur and pink eyes, were bouncing around their cage. It wasn't long before they were chewing on alfalfa hay and tasting the rolled barley.

Then came the only part of raising rabbits that I hated from the first time I was required to do it, until we moved four or five years later. Someone had to kill and "dress" the half-grown rabbits so my mother could have the meat fried, and ready for dinner when milking was completed.

It meant that I left the milking activity for ten minutes, selected and killed a young rabbit of frying size, skinned and cleaned it, and then delivered it to my mother. I must have done this a hundred times, but always felt some guilt when having to take a rabbit's life. Rabbit meat became a favorite of most of us, as I remember.

Occasionally my father would kill and butcher a male calf that weighed 150-200 pounds. His deal with the landowner was that the landowner would get all of the female (heifer) calves, to raise them to milking age. Half of the male, bull calves went to each, my father and the landowner. Several times a year we had veal for dinners, and for a while it meant veal every night or every other night. We didn't freeze meat but did have a refrigerator that kept fresh meat available for two to three weeks.

* * * * *

I think I first fell in love when I was in the sixth grade and my blue eyed, blonde neighbor was in the fourth grade. Pearl was a pretty girl with a bright smile. I just couldn't see another girl in the whole school.

My brother, Roy, handled the girlfriend thing much better than I did. He loved a lot of girls and many of them seemed to love him. I just never figured out what girls wanted. It came easy for Roy.

Pearl wasn't the best student. When she got into the fifth grade, and thus came into the same big classroom as my brother and I, it became her fate to receive the ire of Miss Potter, who expected everyone to do well. I almost cried when Pearl was asked to go to the blackboard to work out an assigned problem and couldn't get the answer.

Pearl never acknowledged or returned my affection. Maybe she wasn't ready for boys. Most of the other students teased me about "loving Pearl." It must have been rather apparent.

For the three years until I graduated from the eighth grade, Valentine's Day had to be my special torment. My mother bought us kits of stuff for making valentines, including some paper lace. I never would admit that I put a special effort into the valentine I made for Pearl, but I obviously did. When that great day came, I always waited expectantly for her to tell me how wonderful she thought my valentine was, but it never happened.

Often, in summers, my father flood-irrigated our front lawn on Sunday mornings. He never had to ask me twice to help. I was out front working or pretending to be busy so I could wave to Pearl and her family as they drove by our house on the way to church.

Pearl and her year-older sister, Elaine, occasionally came to visit or play games with us. Roy and I sometimes walked the quarter-mile to their farm home. Their parents also ran a dairy, one that they owned.

I think it irked my father a little that Pearl's father ran a dairy almost the size of ours, but all by himself. They only had the two girls and neither went near the barns.

On these infrequent visits I tried to be very casual, but it wasn't the way I felt.

Ray Union School and Miss Potter

Getting in trouble at Ray School during my fifth through eighth grades was something I tried to avoid. I worked hard and followed school rules carefully. Only twice do I remember getting reprimanded seriously by Miss Potter.

The first episode came about when I was in the sixth grade. Most of the playground equipment, bars, swings, the slide and teeter-totter were located under trees in one corner of the school yard. The most-prized piece of equipment, the "giant stride," quite like a May Pole, was positioned in an open area closer to the main school building. Eight chains hung from a rotating cap at the top of the heavy iron pipe, which was anchored in the ground with hundreds of pounds of concrete.

Handholds at the end of the chains allowed up to eight students to start running around the pole and then to all take giant strides as they whirled in a big circle. The "giant stride" was hardly ever idle during recesses or lunch hour.

One recess a group of us "older" boys wanted to use the giant stride but it was being used by the girls in the younger grades. We asked repeatedly for a turn before the bell rang ending the recess. The younger girls kept saying, "Pretty soon," but showed no signs of relinquishing the favored equipment.

All of the girls wore dresses or skirts. It wasn't long before one of us boys, perhaps me, figured out a way to gain access to the giant stride. "Let's tell the girls we can see their underpants!"

It worked! The girls let go of the handles of the giant stride, immediately. But instead of looking for other activities they headed for their classroom on a run!

Our turn at the giant stride lasted only a minute or two and Miss Potter showed up looking awfully stern. Her lecture likely lasted only five minutes, but long enough to insure that we boys didn't again try to get turns on the giant stride by reminding the girls we could identify the color of their panties.

Another incident, when I was in the eighth grade, really brought on the wrath of Miss Potter. Two brothers in the seventh grade were of Japanese ancestry. I liked both of them a lot and they were always part of all the school activities. For some reason they told my brother Roy and me, and the other boy in our class, Jack, how to say some "bad" words in Japanese. It was an immediate hit. We went around the school yard repeating all of the newly-learned words and expressions. Miss Potter apparently caught on rather quickly. It wasn't long before she called the two Japanese boys into the school room and asked exactly what those words she was hearing meant.

Ko and his brother Akira were honest boys and shortly Jack, Roy and I were asked to have a private session with Miss Potter.

I vividly remember what she said to each of us. "Jack, I'm disappointed but I have to admit I might have expected something like this from you."

"From you, Roy, something silly, yes, but never this."

"Kenneth, I can't believe this of you at all, and am totally disappointed."

It was comforting that Miss Potter never carried the event any further. Roy and I waited in dread for several days for a follow-up explosion from my father, but our teacher chose not to inform our parents.

As each class of students came near the end of the eighth grade, Miss Potter gave each member a mathematical problem that she felt would be a real challenge. She asked that we not get parental help.

Roy and I likely would have been able to solve the difficult problem, but we also knew our father was awfully good in math. We just couldn't help but suggest he give us "hints."

Those hints, of course, led to a fairly easy solution. Our teacher said we were among the very few eighth graders who had ever solved her special problem. It was with reluctance that we told Miss Potter we had a tiny bit of help from our father.

* * * * *

Money was never plentiful at our house. The milk checks from the creamery averaged $35-$45 every two weeks. With chickens, rabbits, occasional veal and beef, milk, cream for making butter, and lots of garden space, we had a good start on food. Fresh oranges cost $1 for a 50-pound box. My mother made all of our bread.

By contrast, Miss Potter was paid $150 a month. The depression we were in seemingly didn't affect public employees as severely as many farmers or privately-employed people. My father never made an issue of Miss Potter's nice salary. We children were admonished never to mention it. My father liked and respected her. As an honor student himself in school, he recognized the huge effort she put out to teach all subjects (except music) to four class levels.

I never felt we were poor. We always had lots of beans and bread, mashed potatoes and gravy, a cooked vegetable, and often some meat. Fried eggs were there for the asking at breakfast, to go along with the regularly-eaten cold cereal and milk. We boys went barefooted to school right up through the eighth grade and were the only ones at school to do so. We looked at going barefoot as a matter of choice. My father was adamant against taking charity and always prided himself in our independence from it.

He was, of course, always looking for ways to earn an extra few dollars. Cutting and selling firewood for kitchen stoves was the method most often used. One neighbor had a grove of eucalyptus trees that grew rapidly and made excellent though fast-burning firewood when split and dried. The neighbor, Mr. Williams, gave us the trees free as long as we did all of the work, kept him in firewood, and burned all of the trash afterwards. He and my father thought a lot of each other. Some years later, my father, older brother and I were asked to be pallbearers at Mr. William's funeral. We were teenagers then.

Many summer and fall days, and on weekends, my brothers and I helped my father fall the trees, then split and tier the finished foot-long sticks of wood for drying. A tier of cookstove wood measured eight feet long, four feet high, and the length of the individual sticks, one foot across.

Cookstove firewood at 50¢ per tier sold quite easily. It had to be left stacked in one tier lots for a couple of summer months to dry. I remember being somewhat annoyed with my father because he always insisted we put some extra firewood on each tier "so the customer would get full measure." My brother and I knew how much of our labor went into each tier of finished wood. We felt our customers already got more than full value for their 50¢.

By putting in a full day, starting after completing the morning dairy work, and ending in time to begin evening milking, we could split and stack up to five tiers of wood, which eventually would earn us about $2.50.

* * * * *

One wood-cutting project was a financial disaster from the start. A neighbor, also a dairyman, had pulled out five acres of old grape vines and had planted clover pasture for his dairy cattle.

With his small tractor he had dragged all of the gnarled vines into a dry area near his house and stacked them about four feet high. The pile was probably 80 to 100 feet long and about 20 feet across.

This neighbor was aware that my father had a big buzz saw and one day asked him what he would charge to cut all of the dead grape vines into pieces of firewood not over a foot in length. This would fit his family cookstove and provide them several years of hot-burning wood.

My father was proud of his big circular saw. It was thirty inches in diameter and could easily cut logs up to a foot in diameter. My father was an accomplished farm mechanic. The power came from a big Buick automobile engine anchored to an old vehicle chassis. The pulley from the engine was connected to the pulley on the circular saw by an endless belt. With the saw blade turning as fast as several thousand rpm's the foot-diameter logs were cut through in seconds!

The saw blade frightened me when it turned at a high rate. I could see the outer edge of the huge 30" blade move sideways close to half an inch as it screamed around, waiting for a log to be pushed against it. My father was fearless and seemed to be casual as he put logs into position for cutting. The blade never flew apart into a million pieces so I guess my fears were groundless. Hundreds of times, though, I held my breath and just hoped.

Having this marvelous saw must have prompted my father to make the unbelievable bid he did make to our neighbor. He offered to cut up the entire pile of old grape vines for $5.

I remember several times over the many years when my mother would remark, "Your father always thinks he can do a big job in much less time than it really will take." We were all aghast when my father announced we were going to take a day or two and earn $5 for cutting up the immense pile of iron-hard grape vines.

But $5 was bid and my father would absolutely never go back on his word! The big buzz saw was towed into place and the cutting began. My brother and I brought the big, awkward vines, often weighing 40 to 50 pounds to the saw. My father hoisted the vines onto the saw platform and did the cutting. Many vines had to be re-positioned on the platform half a dozen times to cut off the many limbs that had grown out in all directions.

After a day we hadn't made a dent in the pile. My father had never before cut dry grape wood with his saw. The wood must have been "as hard as rock" because the teeth on the saw became dull within two hours. Everything had to stop while my father took an hour or two to re-sharpen the hundred saw teeth with a hand file. It must have taken ten part days of sawing, with three of us working to cut that huge pile of grape vines. The gasoline costs alone ate up much of the $5.

My father didn't seem to like this neighbor very much for reasons he never explained. He liked him a lot less afterwards! I overheard my father comment to my mother several times that surely this man would see the magnitude of the cutting job and offer to give us more than the agreed $5. He didn't, though, and my father was far too proud and stubborn to ask for more than the agreed amount.

* * * * *

I was completely overwhelmed when, after several months of living and working on the dairy, my father called us all together and announced that each child was going to regularly receive part of the milk check from the creamery. It was wonderful! Our early morning and night tasks were to be recognized and rewarded. I can't remember how much my brother, Roy, and I received, or what went to our younger brothers or sister, but I know I thought it was generous. It could have been 5¢ or 25¢ or even 35¢. How much can parents give when the monthly check couldn't have been over $75-$90? This wonderful situation continued every month for as long as we operated the dairy.

Changes and More Changes

Disaster struck from a direction none of us anticipated, probably about three years after we moved to the dairy. The Health Department, whether local or state, announced that all Grade B dairies were to have all cows tested for bovine tuberculosis. Grade A dairies selling raw milk were on this program already, but milk, like ours, that was pasteurized before use, had not had such a requirement.

Our cows seemed completely healthy. They weren't coughing or losing milk production. How could there be anything wrong with our cows? I remember the worried discussions by my parents. It seemed that bovine tuberculosis couldn't be passed on to humans. That was reassuring because we all worked closely around the cows. We regularly drank the milk raw. There was some concern about what it would all mean to us.

It was an exciting and worrisome day when the men arrived to do the scheduled testing. Rumors were flying around that some dairies were losing half of their herds based on testing results.

We herded our cows into the milking sections of the big barn and locked them into their stantions. They were given a little alfalfa hay to help reduce their nervousness at this unusual happening.

The two veterinarians raised each cow's tail and injected a solution with a hypodermic needle into the underside base of the animal's tail. When it was all completed the vets said they would be back in 72 hours to "read" the results. We were to milk the cows as normal and were not to disturb the underside of each animal's tail where the injection had been made. Apparently the bovine tuberculosis showed up as a small, hard lump where the injection of serum had been made.

The day came and again we herded our cows into their milking areas. We watched in disbelief as one after another of our best-milking cows were painted with big red X's, showing that they had tested positive for TB.

Almost half of the herd of animals was lost. For several days we watched in further disbelief as my father helped load the diseased cows into a "tallow-wagon." They were headed for processing into dog food!

The dairy owner's loss was far greater than ours. We had immediately lost half of our family income. He had lost a big investment in his herd. There were probably discussions between my father and the land owner, though I don't recall this happening.

The required clean-up took many days, with my brother and I working alongside my father. All feeding and standing areas in the barn had to be hosed and scrubbed clean down to bare wood or concrete! Then a strong lye solution was swabbed over every inch of surface as a disinfectant. This was allowed to stand for several hours and then the areas scrubbed and hosed down again.

Piles of manure and bedding straw that had accumulated had to be spread out onto open pasture areas to be exposed to sunlight. It was a rather miserable job for all of us, but the milking chores were cut in half. I remember pieces of conversation between my parents about what we could do to recover some of the family income. Apparently the landowner had decided to not immediately replace the lost animals. Prices for cows had increased because so many replacement animals were needed.

* * * * *

It wasn't long afterwards until my father announced that he was going to apply for an outside job to help earn money. I was probably twelve by then and Roy was thirteen-and-a-half. If my father was successful in getting the job, Roy and I were to take over most of the milking, feeding, and cleaning the barns. It was kind of exciting and scary at the same time.

The job opening was for a helper in a water-well drilling company in Lodi, about ten miles from our place. My father knew he could handle the job. He was young, strong and a good practical mechanic. He was certain he could stand the hard, often cold work and still come home after eight hours and help finish the evening dairy work.

The job would pay $75 a month, working a full day, five days a week. It would better than double our family income if he could land the job.

My father announced that he had figured out an almost sure way he could win out over all of the other men applying for the job. He would offer to work completely free for a full week. If his work wasn't fully satisfactory, the company owed him nothing. If they liked his work, he was to get the job. It was an exciting thought, and an unheard of approach, but our situation was desperate.

At the end of that next week my father had the job. He wasn't very popular at first with some of the other men because they felt it demeaning that a man would give his work free just to land a job. My father acknowledged later that he hoped the well-drilling company would compensate him partially for the "free week," but they didn't. He had made the offer. They had accepted it. My father worked steadily at helping to drill water-wells for a period of one or two years.

My brother and I saw very little of my father around the dairy barn during the weekdays. The well-drilling work was hard, cold and demanding. He required some extra rest to be able to handle his job.

Roy and I probably did a fair job with the cow milking, the feeding and the cleaning of the barn, without regular supervision. We were beginning high school and would arrive home by 3:30 each afternoon. I do recall that tempers flared occasionally and my brother and I would end up throwing half-buckets of milk at each other.

* * * * *

A bicycle for Roy and me had been the promise my father made if we would really pitch in and help with the firewood operations.

One summer evening after work he came home with two fabulous bicycles. My brother's had cost $15, and had wide handlebars. Mine had cost $17.50 and had straight-back handlebars. Both bicycles had shiny new pedals. It was a dream come true!

Roy and I leaped on our bikes and soon were roaring up and down the county road to our mother's admonition to be careful.

Fifteen minutes later we were both home, pushing our bicycles. We had crashed head-on! Both were accusing the other of having been at fault. I was crying, Roy was angry. We were absolutely destroyed; our parents couldn't believe that our rewards for a summer's wood-cutting lasted only fifteen minutes.

My bicycle was most heavily damaged. The "fork" was pushed back so far that nothing worked. The front wheel was badly bent.

Roy's bicycle had a badly bent wheel and a flat tire. My mother worked over our scratches and bruises. My father stared at the broken bicycles. He could see that front wheels on both bicycles had to be replaced. The expensive "fork" on my bike would have to also be replaced.

My father's words were final. "Boys, you may not have your bicycles for a long time. There is no money to have them repaired." As I remember it was over six months before our bicycles were fixed. No amount of pleading changed the situation.

It would have cost close to half of a two-week milk paycheck to pay for two new bicycle wheels and a new "fork" for one bike. My father was correct in his decision to wait on the repair until some money could be accumulated.

Roy and I didn't need the bicycles. There were no stores to ride to on errands for our parents. The school bus picked us up and dropped us off right in front of the house.

We didn't have friends who expected us to ride over occasionally. I guess it made sense to go without our bicycles until a later date. It was a sad pair of boys, though, who had to accept the loss of their reward for all of the wood-cutting done the past couple of summers.

My father locked the broken bicycles up in the "tank-house" and that was that.

* * * * *

Several expressions and verses by my father made quite an impact on me. One in particular I believe he used to annoy my mother.

> "When I asked her to wed,
> she very politely said,
> 'Go see father.'
> Now she knew that I knew
> that her father was dead;
> And she knew that I knew
> what a life he had led.
> So she knew that I knew
> what she meant when she said,
> 'Go see father.' "

Another I have was used occasionally when someone commented, "Oh, he is a has been."

"I'd rather be a has been than a might have been, by far, for a might have been has never been, while a has been was once an 'are.' "

My father was a scholar and a stickler for correct speech. In a mountainous area where small riverlets are everywhere, creeks that run year-round are named for an early landowner or for an animal spotted there, etc. Lots of the local people called them "cricks." My father's response to that was, "He who for creek says crick has been seek for the past wick."

On the other hand it didn't faze him one bit to sound the "L's" in "almond" and "salmon." "After all," my father said, "if the L's were meant to be silent, they would have been spelled without the L's to begin with." Logic was generally on my father's side.

* * * * *

When my older brother and I were sophomores in high school our parents told us that they had completed plans to move. They had purchased the cows and Grade A raw milk processing equipment from two small dairies. They were taking over the lease of a small ranch where one of these dairymen was operating. It was a huge change for all of us, because now milk had to be handled in a totally hygienic manner and delivered in glass bottles to individual homes and a few small stores.

I never asked where the money came from to buy out these two small dairy operations. No doubt my parents had saved some of the income from my father's water-well drilling job. I overheard my father talking about a California World War I Veteran's bonus. Years later after my father's death, my mother told me part of it came from the sale of a small residential lot left to her by her father. In his will he had left a similar piece of ground to each of the other three children, hopeful, I guess, that each would choose to build a home and thus keep all of his family close by.

Two weeks hadn't passed before another change jolted our family. My father had asked my brother to quit high school and do the needed work of washing milk bottles, hosing and scrubbing the barn, running the sterilizer for the milking equipment and bottles, and taking the animals to and from the pasture. My father would handle the morning and evening milk routes and supervise the milking.

My brother just shrugged his shoulders and said it was okay with him. I don't think I ever felt so lonely in my life when I took off for school alone. In one day Roy had become the second man in our family. He adjusted as though it was just the normal thing to do. Our bicycles had been repaired by this time and I continued to ride mine to and from high school, about two or three miles.

Roy and I had done well in our woodshop classes. This was our second year and our teacher had approved our building a twelve-foot row boat. At the time my brother quit school we were well along on the "blueprints" and diagrams required to be approved before construction began. My father had agreed to pay for the spruce wood needed for the project.

I was overwhelmed! Up to now Roy and I had worked together. Suddenly there was no one to ask, "Does this look right?" "Is this the correct angle for rib #3?"

Obviously it was too big of a project for one student to complete during the balance of the school year. Not much can be done during just one hour each day, which had to include set-up and clean-up time.

I'll never understand why my woodshop teacher approved my going ahead alone. I must have wanted to pretty badly.

Mr. Crose, the teacher, gave me a big boost right off when he saw how determined I was to prove that I could finish the rowboat within the year. He gave me, free, a locust prow for my boat, already completely chiseled into shape. The insets for the siding were already cut out. Mr. Crose explained that another student had abandoned his boat project after having constructed the prow. With that magnificent prow I could visualize a boat so strong that it could hit headlong into a concrete wall without any damage.

My first major error was to mis-figure the exact angles of the ten ribs that made the boat's frame. How I did that I don't know, but several days were needed to re-calculate the angles and re-drill and re-bolt the ribs. I never even dared tell my teacher. I just re-did everything as I pretended things were going smoothly.

My second catastrophe came about when I realized that two six-inch wide spruce boards for the siding had been cut a foot short. There was no way I was going to ask my father to put out more money for two new boards, each over twelve feet long. Although I knew I'd be teased about my mistake for years, I decided to splice a short piece of board onto the ends of the boards cut too short, and hope the error wouldn't make the boat leak.

It was a scary but proud day when my father took my three brothers and me for our first ride in the river that bordered our ranch. My boat never got it's coat of varnish or paint and became waterlogged and heavy, but we used it many times until it finally sank in a little lagoon adjacent to the river.

* * * * *

After less than a year at our little leased ranch my father made a down payment on a big 100-acre ranch west of Lodi, also bordering the Mokelumne River. In a way I hated to leave the place we were renting and starting the Grade A raw milk daily operation. I loved the smell of the corn silage as we forked it down to the cows during that winter. We had a wonderful beach for swimming during the summer we lived there. Roy and I became really skilled at swinging out on a long rope over the river and doing a perfect dive into the fast-flowing water. Once in a while we let the current take us downstream into the deeper water. Only by swimming vigorously could we avoid being pulled under by the big whirlpool near the pump drawing water to irrigate our animal pastures.

Here too, I learned to like fried frog's legs. During April the river level raised and flooded a swampy area. By May the frogs became active and their croaking could be heard all through the swamp, some places five or ten feet deep in water.

Sometimes with the help of a BB gun and sometimes just by sneaking up carefully, we captured the big frogs. My mother was at first reluctant to fry them but soon several of us couldn't imagine how any meat could taste any better.

The move to our owned ranch was something we had never dreamed of. The house was old but suitable for our family. Roy and I were assigned to live in a little out-building located thirty feet from the main house. It also served as the washroom for my mother and had running water but no bathroom.

My father had a new dairy barn erected on the ranch plus a concrete watering trough for the cows. A big hay barn already was on the property. The move of ten miles was made smoothly and for the second time my parents were attempting to become owners of their own place.

By this time my two younger brothers were helping with the milking. One brother, Harold, accompanied my father on the night milk delivery, leaving about 8:00 P.M. and getting home about 10:30 P.M. I never felt it was fair that Harold had to stay up that late, but he never complained. He was allowed to sleep in for an extra hour the next morning. He helped with the regular milking at night after school.

My older brother, Roy, was over 16 by then, and carried on most of the daytime work not done by my father. He didn't comment much about the situation but I sensed that things weren't exactly right between my father and Roy. Occasionally I picked up pieces of short but heated arguments between them.

My Brother Leaves

Our new ranch had ten acres of grapes, mostly Tokays, and all delivered each year to a local winery. My father contracted with a local man to harvest and deliver the grapes to the winery.

Someone had to pick the grapes and my father said Roy and I could be part of the man's picking crew as long as it didn't interfere with our milking and dairy chores.

The contractor paid five cents for us to pick a fifty-pound box of grapes and to stack the full boxes. Some weekends we could pick as many as 50 boxes. Every spare hour during harvest we ran out to pick the grapes. Roy always outdid me but I could keep close to his picking speed.

Sometime after the harvest was over and the contractor had paid both Roy and me, Roy said that my father had asked if he could borrow the money and Roy had given it to him. I told Roy that my father wasn't about to have my money, and that I was going to spend mine for some clothes. Except for the corduroy pants bought for school each year, neither of us had any "dress" clothes and no money to buy any with.

After several months Roy was telling me that my father didn't give him back the money he had borrowed and he didn't think that was fair at all. Neither did I, but I still had my money and wasn't about to part with it. Roy didn't make a big issue about it, but I knew he and my father weren't feeling good about their relationship. I was starting my junior year in high school so was at home only during non-school hours.

One day when I got home from school on the bus, my father asked if I knew where my older brother was. Apparently, when my father had returned home about noon from the milk route, he found Roy gone, along with the family sedan.

My father was positive I was in on the run-away scheme. I knew nothing of it but could not convince my father of that. Roy and I were so close that he just knew I was in on the scheme.

My father was furious! He was going to tell the police that Roy had stolen the family car. It wasn't a pleasant few hours!

My mother was frightened and cried a lot. Her concern was that Roy would be safe. She wanted to hear from him and know that he was okay, even if he wouldn't come home. She convinced my father not to call the police. Somehow we got through the milking that night and the next morning.

My mind was in turmoil. After my father left the next morning for the milk delivery route and I had completed washing bottles, running the sterilizer and finishing urgent chores, I told my mother I was going to quit school and take my older brother's place. She had no argument because she saw no other way out.

By mid-morning I was on the way to school to check out, running, walking or trotting the twenty miles to and from school. By early afternoon I was home, no longer a student. I felt good, I'm sure, about being able to fill in, but uncertain about having to quit school during the early part of my junior year, and maybe never finishing.

I became the "boss" of the milking operations. My father occasionally came to the barn to see how things were going. My two younger brothers, Donald and Harold, were beginning high school and helped regularly in the milking. Harold continued to accompany my father on evening milk route deliveries. My mother continued to openly worry about what might have happened to Roy.

It must have been four to six months later that a relative about 300 miles from our place wrote to my mother to tell her he had seen Roy delivering milk to a local creamery for a big dairyman in the area. I'm not sure who was more relieved, my mother or me. I'd always felt that my brother had done his part to help the family business. It was his right to try to do something on his own if that was what he chose. It did bother me some that he hadn't found a way to let my mother know that he was safe.

My mother never learned to drive. My father had continued to be upset about losing the family car and having to use the delivery truck to transport his family around.

Within a week my mother and two women friends, both drivers, left for the 300-mile trip north to try and locate my brother, Roy, and, if possible, return the vehicle. By asking around they apparently located the little cabin where Roy was living. Mother told me later that she walked alone up to the cabin and knocked. She said Roy opened the door, said, "Oh, hi Mom," and showed no surprise.

He had purchased his own car. Our family car was in the yard. One of the women drove it home. No doubt my mother asked about Roy's returning home but that didn't occur. He was completely happy with being independent and wanted to stay that way.

My mother brought back word that Roy had found an immediate job on a large dairy in the Ferndale area. His experience on our family dairies had allowed him to fit in as a full-time employee. He was being paid a man's wages and doing the work of a man. Roy never had a lot of money to spend and, except for his car, had been saving most of his earnings.

* * * * *

Shortly after that, my father bought me a car, a 1929 Chevrolet sedan. He paid $50 for it. I was completely delighted with my new freedom. I don't remember using it a whole lot, but I washed it regularly. Having it made the long hours and constant dairy work more acceptable.

Occasionally former school friends came out to the ranch to see me. We would sit on the bed in my outbuilding and play cards. The evening always ended too soon as my mother insisted that I be in bed by 10:00 P.M. even on weekends. It did provide a welcome opportunity to keep in touch with four or five friends.

Most probably my car was used on weekend drives with my younger brothers and their friends. Though not outstanding students my brothers continued on in high school but worked along with me doing the dairy work and helping with weekend hauling hay and needed chores. We had a good relationship.

We used the car to occasionally go to the Friday night high school football games when they were played at "home." I remember the heavy fog encountered driving home from November games. I would ask one of my brothers to run alongside the car so they could alert me to oncoming cars or to cars overtaking us in the fog. My little Chevy was rather noisy and I wanted some advance warning so I could get off the narrow pavement. My mother worried constantly when we were out late in some of that intense fog.

During my sophomore year I had taken an auto-mechanics class along with woodshop so I had some idea, though not much interest, in how an engine worked.

It was my friends who convinced me after the football season that I should overhaul my car. They would help! My father was agreeable and said he would pay for any needed parts! He said I could use ten feet at one end of the feeding area of the hay barn to lay out the parts of the engine as we took it apart.

It was really an adventure. I never thought there could be so many small parts to a simple four-cylinder engine. I never lacked for willing hands. My father paid to have the valve "seats" in the "head" professionally redone and bought needed piston rings and gaskets.

Putting the engine back together went smoothly and the big day came a month or so later when I was ready to give the crank a turn. The engine started right off! It stopped or we turned it off after a few minutes and someone suggested we check the oil level.

The oil was four inches too high on the oil stick and foamy. It took only a minute to realize that water from the engine block and radiator had run down into the oil.

We had left water in the block. It had frozen during the severe cold in December and the block had cracked.

The engine, of course, was ruined and I was without a car. My father sympathized with my situation but there was nothing to change it.

* * * * *

Whether it was because of my request, my mother's, or his own idea I don't remember, but my brother Roy said he would be agreeable to coming home and working on the dairy so I could resume school. I was embarrassed about returning to high school as a junior, now a full year behind my original class. I couldn't pass it up however.

Roy stuck with it almost through the school year. It was an uneasy truce between my father and him, but it worked for me. I would catch the school bus at the end of our private lane or ride with my father as he got underway on his morning milk route. I would run the bottles of milk up to the porches of our customers until time came for him to drop me off in front of the high school.

I didn't mind helping but soon came to realize the inevitable would happen. My father would say, "Let's do just one more house," and I would be five or ten minutes late to the first period class.

After a half dozen such situations, the attendance office would no longer give me an admittance slip. They sent me to see the Dean of Men, a Mr. Jim Conklin. During the year he and I became well-acquainted but he never once questioned my explanation for being tardy. Mr. Conklin said he remembered my father as an excellent student. I guess he thought there was no harm in letting things go on as they were. He was experienced enough to know when, and when not to make an issue of things that couldn't be easily changed.

* * * * *

My junior year went along fairly uneventfully. Along the way I fell in love with a girl in my English class. I'll always be able to understand fully a teenager being in love. It was a feeling beyond anything I had ever experienced. We found ways to meet for a minute between classes and held hands walking down the halls. Other students must have felt we were "nuts" but my whole world evolved around this girl, Lacia, and her smile.

It all ended through her decision, not mine. One day as I walked through a classroom, I noticed a letter had been dropped on the floor. It had been opened and had the return address of my girlfriend. Out of curiosity I glanced at the letter and found that it was about me.

She was telling a girlfriend that she had met this really nice boy and that she knew he liked her a lot. Lacia told her friend, though, that she had a regular boyfriend and now didn't know how to tell me that she just wanted to be a friend, nothing more.

I felt totally empty. It slowly dawned on me that someone had purposefully dropped the letter where I would see it. After an overnight of worrying about my loss, and deciding I couldn't change things, I gave Lacia her letter the next morning, explaining that I had found it. I guess she could tell by the look on my face that I had read the contents. Nothing much needed to be said and it must have been a rather silent good-bye.

* * * * *

Early in my junior year I proposed another project for my woodshop teacher's approval. Mr. Crose listened attentively but was reluctant to see me take on a major undertaking like building a full-sized office desk. Without doubt he had a vivid memory of my sophomore-year spruce boat that he had released without any varnish or paint work. Mr. Crose was adamant about work being completed before he released it.

I guess I convinced him that my father needed an office desk so he gave in. Building a four-drawer desk looked like a reasonable project to me. After all, hadn't I constructed a twelve-foot spruce boat that floated?

My desk-building went well except that time ran out again. Drawers proved to be especially difficult to fit exactly. An eighth on an inch too wide wouldn't fit and an eighth of an inch too narrow wasn't acceptable to my teacher.

Finally, everything was glued and fitted but early June had arrived and the sanding and varnishing, probably two weeks work with the limited school hours, hadn't been done. My teacher wanted to hold the desk over until the following year but between my father and my pleadings, the desk was released.

My promise to sand and finish the desk at home was part of our agreement, but that wasn't lived up to. My father immediately loaded up the desk and filled the drawers. He had to get monthly invoices and statements out to his milk customers, so completing my desk was delayed and eventually forgotten.

Structurally, my desk was put together very well. My father used it regularly until it was destroyed in a home fire many years later.

I had no regrets or apologies to make for my unfinished spruce boat or pine office desk. There were no other boats or desks even attempted during the three years I took woodshop classes.

It wasn't that I didn't try to get these big projects finished. Instead of visiting with my friends during the half-hour after school and before the buses left, I raced down to the woodshop and made all the progress I could. Time just ran out!

One regret I did have was not learning to use a lathe. I would envy the boys turning out mahogany or cherry wood lamps that I knew would look just great in our home. I could see nothing difficult about it — just make sure your long piece of wood was centered exactly in the lathe.

Using the lathe tools to get a beautiful design was something I knew I could do, but never tried.

* * * * *

Along towards the end of my junior year, my brother Roy announced that he was going back to Humboldt County and resume his independent life. No one questioned his decision. Roy had made a major contribution to my being able to complete my junior year.

On our dairy he had a certain amount of weekend freedom. He and I had several mutual friends who occasionally came over for card games or touch-football. He had some money earned during his year away to go to occasional movies. His car was his real pride, as he had bought and paid for it on his own.

With my younger brothers' increasing help with the dairy, things seemed to run effectively. Before many months my father bought a second car for me, a 1937 Chevrolet sedan. It was a beautiful blue car that cost $350. I felt like a king driving it. Although most times I continued catching the bus, on occasion I would drive my car to school during my senior year

My life at school took on an entire new meaning when I enrolled in a journalism class. After a few weeks, our weekly school paper took on a much higher level of interest. I watched the second-year journalism students bring in articles, write headlines and paste up the paper. It seemed to me to be a tremendously important job.

I found out that everything had to be put together and delivered Thursday afternoon to the local newspaper office. They would do the typesetting and printing of the four-page paper and deliver the finished product back to the school by noon Friday. I watched students line up Friday afternoon for their copy and imagined how great it would be to have something I had written printed.

I quickly learned how to write headlines for stories and articles. I must have turned in a few stories about school sports because our teacher told me she was going to name me as the "Assistant Sports Editor." I couldn't believe it. My name was going to appear in print on the masthead of our school paper!

That paper became the highlight of my senior year's activity. With my car I could work at school an extra two hours and get home just in time to join my younger brothers in the evening's work. I would lie in bed and write stuff for the paper until my mother called and reminded me that I absolutely had to turn off the light and go to bed.

My greatest success had to be the sports page for the spring Senior Issue. My assignment was to identify and write an article about the outstanding senior in every sport on campus.

After interviews with each coach (who made the selections) I wrote the dozen or so articles.

I worked at night trying to hide my light from my mother's eyes. In all there were 162 column-inches of finished print.

I wasn't aware at the time that I had a severe Pterygium problem in one eye. It was an endless source of jokes among my friends. "Those red eyes meant Ken has been drinking." It wasn't funny to me as the one eye felt like it was being rubbed with sandpaper much of the time.

Tragedy on the Farm

Our family situation changed early in the summer between my junior and senior year.

A family with five children, some who attended school with my brothers and me, lived several miles from us. Their economic situation was dismal. It was rumored that an alcohol problem could have been involved.

I'm not certain how it all came about. Possibly the 16-year-old boy asked my mother if he could live with us. Maybe my mother had heard of the family's dire situation and had asked the boy's mother if there was something she might do to help. That would have been my mother's style. Somehow, too, we knew that the boy wasn't getting along well with his father.

Lonzo arrived with a bundle of clothes, his total life's belongings. My father had cleaned out a small cabin several hundred feet from our house and not too distant from the milk barn. We had used the building to store seeds and specialty feed supplements for the animals. The building had a raised wooden floor and several windows, plus a sink and running water. It must have been used for living quarters by a previous owner of our ranch.

It seemed like a good arrangement. Lonzo had dropped out of school and was adamant about not returning. He was to do limited work and chores in return for his food and lodging. My mother gladly included his clothes washing with that of her own children.

I'm sure my father didn't pay Lonzo any salary. None of my brothers or I were any longer given any pay or allowance. It is possible that my father occasionally gave him a few dollars. I don't know.

Having Lonzo to wash and sterilize the milk bottles and equipment allowed me to continue on to school. He would assist my father in some other farm work but didn't learn to milk cows. My two younger brothers and I could readily milk the 30-35 cows my parents owned. Because Lonzo didn't milk it wasn't critical that he arrive at the milk barn at 5:00 A.M. as my younger brothers and I did. One of us would give him a wake-up call as we headed for the barn.

Often Lonzo went right back to sleep. Because we needed to work rapidly to set up filtering, cooling and bottling equipment, as well as washing the cows udders to prepare them for milking, it was often forty-five minutes before one of us again gave Lonzo a wake-up knock and call. I could understand why he saw little need to climb out of bed, especially on cold mornings. My brothers and I really needed no help. By working rapidly we could complete the milking, processing, bottling and loading the milk truck within the time we had.

My father, though, became really annoyed when on occasion he came to the milk barn and found Lonzo still in bed or just arriving. Other than that I probably would have been content for him to be available only after the morning milking was completed. I'm not sure that Lonzo had even accompanied my father, brothers and me on the most recent required trip to the County Health

Department laboratory. All active employees in Grade A milk operations were required to have urine, stool and physical examinations twice yearly to check for communicable diseases.

Lonzo appeared to participate in the daytime work assigned by my father without complaint. Two of his brothers would often come by on weekends. We weren't close friends but everyone seemed to get along well. There was no discussion of Lonzo wanting to return home. On most Sunday mornings following completion of the milk route delivery, he would accompany us to church. His social life as a teenager was limited to the few things he did with my family. Parties just weren't a part of any of my family's daily activities. We worked, we ate, we slept. My brothers, my sister and I went to school. It couldn't have been a completely fulfilling life for a 15-16 year-old boy watching our activities mostly from the sidelines.

Then it happened! I had taken the morning milk route while my father stayed on the ranch. It may have been a Saturday or I may have stayed out of school for the day.

When I completed the bottle delivery and drove up our lane to the milk barn a police car was waiting. Lonzo was dead and they wanted to know of my possible involvement.

My father had discovered Lonzo's body at mid-morning when he went to the milk barn to see how the equipment, bottle-washing and sterilizing was coming along. Lonzo had been killed by a single shot from my .22 caliber rifle that I used for hunting squirrels and cottontail rabbits. The police said the end of the gun barrel had been placed under Lonzo's chin and apparently fired by pushing the trigger with a three-foot stick lying nearby. The bullet had entered Lonzo's brain and he died right there.

I hoped for a long time that it was an accident. Maybe Lonzo had pulled the gun out of it's accustomed corner by the barrel. If he unintentionally bounced the gun butt on the concrete floor, this could have jarred the gun into firing. He occasionally took my gun for brief squirrel hunting trips along a high levee surrounding part of our ranch. We purposefully didn't keep a bullet in the single-shot rifle but a box of shells was kept nearby.

The police weren't accepting any accident theory as much as I didn't want to believe that Lonzo felt his life was so empty as to take his own life. They were totally satisfied that it was a suicide. Their only interest in me was to see if I could tell them what caused Lonzo to do what he did. I wasn't any help. My waking hours were so jammed with work and school that I can't say I had thought too much about Lonzo's future. Now he had none.

There was some talk about a note being found in which Lonzo penned his disappointment over my younger sister's lack of return of his affections.

I felt even worse for my mother's situation than for his mother's. She had welcomed him into our family and always made sure Lonzo felt good about having his meals with us. She always had his clothes laundered and put in a neat bundle in his cabin. My mother made very sure that Lonzo never felt he was a burden on her. In return he was courteous and always remembered to tell her how good dinner was.

All four of the boys in my family were pallbearers at Lonzo's funeral. Roy returned to his work away from home and the rest of us continued our lives exactly as they had been. Everyone was saddened but hardly knew what to say about Lonzo's tragic ending.

I watched my mother and Lonzo's mother try to comfort each other at the funeral. I began to realize there is nothing so sad as parents losing their children.

My feelings were all over the place. I wanted to go back again and argue with the Lodi Police Chief, a Mr. Jackson, that Lonzo didn't take his own life, that somehow my gun had discharged accidentally.

For weeks I couldn't shake the feeling of guilt. How could I have raced along, with my life jammed so full of activities, and his so empty that he felt worthless?

My father hired an older man to help with the farm work. The man and his wife moved into the cabin where Lonzo had lived. In addition to a place to live, milk and free utilities, my father paid the man $40 a month. It allowed me to often make the morning delivery run as the hired man learned to wash bottles and sterilize the bottles and equipment. My brothers and I saw no point in having this older man learn to milk cows. We kind of liked the guy although he didn't do much work without prodding. My father was occasionally annoyed because of the man's lack of hustle and the difficulty of getting him out of bed in the mornings.

Sports, Woodshop and Graduation

My only try at high school sports was during my senior year. A younger friend and I decided to try out for the lightweight football team or "B" team. My father was adamantly against it. He wouldn't sign the parental consent. I learned when the season was almost over that he had called my high school and threatened to sue them if I played football.

I saw it as my last chance to play on a team. Seniors weren't normally allowed to participate on the "B" team level, but I weighed less than 125 pounds and so fell within the age-weight-height formula. I never missed a practice and would arrive home in time for milking.

Playing was another matter. Our games began at 6:00 P.M. and preceded the 8:00 P.M. varsity game each Friday. Buses for out-of-town games often left the campus at 2:00 P.M. After our "B" team game, all players would dress and then watch the varsity game. Often buses to out-of-town games got everyone back to the campus around midnight. The coach would give each of us fifty cents as we stepped off the bus. Most of us immediately bought a milkshake and hamburger at a late-night shop. The two together cost exactly fifty cents.

Getting back to our ranch posed a problem. An across-the-river neighbor brought his pick-up truck to school. He said he couldn't drive me all the way home but he would gladly take me to the river. Here I would strip and in two trips I could get my clothes and shoes across the river. It required holding stuff in the air with one hand and swimming with the other through the deeper water. Once on the other side I dressed and walked the half mile across our ranch to my cabin. My friend would wait until I was safely across.

It was always a somewhat frightening experience, especially on dark nights and no moon. Late October and early November nights were awfully cold but I soon warmed up again on the walk home.

My younger brothers filled in for me as best they could. Once my father realized I hadn't arrived home from school, he worked along with my brothers.

I always knew a face-off with my father was coming the next day. It always began with, "I thought I told you not to play football." I gritted my teeth and always told him I understood that, but was going to continue anyway. After a few heated threats my father would walk away. I had gotten past one more confrontation.

To say that I had "played football" really overstates the true situation. I practiced regularly, I suited up for every game, but only once was I sent into a game. I lasted one play.

Our "B" football team was having its best year. Not only had we won the first five games that season, we hadn't even been scored upon.

The sixth game was against a small town team a few miles away from Lodi. The varsity didn't play that school because of the difference in school enrollment. Our team that afternoon had already scored. The other team had the ball and my coach sent me in to play left defensive end.

I guess I was overwhelmed, scared, unprepared and inexperienced all packaged into one. I positioned myself too close to the offensive lineman and in seconds after the play began I found my legs locked between the shoulders of the offensive end and tackle. The running back went around my end as though I was standing still because I was. The boy ran all the way for a touchdown, and I was yanked. It was the first and last play for me that season. At 120 pounds I was never sure that I didn't play because of my size or because of the threats my father may have made to school administrators.

* * * * *

Most rewarding to me was the opportunity to play six-man intramural football the following spring. My "B" football coach acted as referee for the entire five-game schedule. Because I had "playing experience" I was named as team captain. It was a wonderful experience for me and our team took second place. We always played right after school and I was able to get home in my car in time for milking. My father either wasn't aware of my after school activities, or chose not to push the issue.

It surely helped my feeling of worthiness when, at the later spring awards assembly, my coach handed me my block letter and introduced me as "end and line backer."

I hadn't been a fast runner but could react quickly. Maybe the coach, in his introduction, remembered that I had picked off several passes in one game.

Could he have remembered too, that as the line-backer in another game, I had made over twenty individual tackles although it was a lost game?

* * * * *

I continued with woodshop classes through my senior year. The teacher, Mr. Crose, recognized me as an accomplished student but did ask that I take on a smaller project than the boat or the office desk of my two prior years.

I selected a magazine table to be made of mahogany. There were to be in-lays around the perimeter of the top and a diamond-shaped inlay in the center of the top. I erred once in a major way. After building the top with mahogany "planks" held together with doweling and glue, I over-used the machine sander. In my attempt to smooth off the top surface, I ground the wood down until the sandpaper dug into the dowelings. That was the end of that table top! It was a pretty embarrassed senior boy who had to ask his father to come up with more money for new mahogany boards to build a new top.

It did turn out well. My teacher asked if he could enter it in the California State Fair for me. It won second place and I received a red ribbon. Mr. Crose even asked me if he could buy it and offered to pay me $25. There was no more proud boy in Lodi High School as I carried that magazine table home.

* * * * *

Sports, Woodshop and Graduation 127

Graduation from high school fitted into just another busy day. We finished the dairy work, had a quick dinner and then all piled into my car for the drive to the high school athletic field for the ceremony.

My father and mother were part of the group as were my two younger brothers and my sister, Yvonne.

Some of the graduating class of about 250 may have worn caps and gowns. I wore a dark pair of trousers, a white shirt and tie. The early June night was pleasant as we lined up on the edge of the football field and received our diplomas.

Immediately afterwards, the graduating class joined everyone else in the adjacent stadium to hear an address by a local business leader. I remember little about his speech except his admonition that we graduates not go out into the world grabbing everything in sight, like hogs at a trough, but to stop along the way and make some contributions to our community. I felt just a little mistreated that the man would liken us to "hogs at a trough."

There was no party, just a quick drive home to get some rest before the 5:00 A.M. wake-up call from my mother the next morning. My father and youngest brother, Harold, still had to make the bottle milk delivery to homes yet that night.

My one graduation gift was from an aunt. She drove out over the weekend and brought me a Tensor lamp. She and my uncle never had children and she always thought we were rather special. She always marveled at the amount of work we did as children. I certainly felt special when she handed me the lamp.

No one could have gotten more use from that bright new lamp than I did. It gave twice the light as the bulb on the end of a cord that I had taped to my iron bed frame.

I spent time many nights designing, cutting out, sanding and finishing mahogany plywood photo albums. Carving out individual letters to position and glue on the cover was a tedious job and one needing good light.

As I remember I gave the finished photo albums to a couple of girls I liked, I guess hoping that might cause them to like me more.

It didn't work out that way and I wondered afterwards about what kind of a fool I was.

* * * * *

My father and I had a workable routine once I was available full-time for work on the dairy.

Both of my brothers and my sister were in high school. They caught the bus at the end of our lane each morning, or rode with my father as he began his milk route.

Yvonne didn't get involved with the dairy chores or milking. Don and I were up first. Harold, because he helped my father with the night delivery route and often didn't get home until 11:00 P.M., slept in for an extra hour. I was worried about Harold because I didn't feel he had enough sleep, but he always showed up at the barn around 6:00 A.M. to join in on completion of the morning work.

Donald and Harold ran for the house about 7:15 A.M. in time to grab breakfast and change clothes for school. I completed what wasn't finished, loaded the milk truck and then went to breakfast. It was a relief to not have to join my brothers and sister in the rush to school.

After breakfast the cows had to be put into the hay barn and locked into their stantions for a feeding of alfalfa hay. While they were eating I washed and sterilized the milk bottles and equipment.

After eating their alfalfa hay the cows were allowed a half hour in lush clover pasture. That activity had to be monitored very rigidly to avoid the animals overeating the clover. They didn't want to leave the green pasture and it often took a lot of shouting and crowding to get the cows back to the corrals.

It both worried and annoyed me when a cow would eat so much clover that she would show signs of bloat. Clover is a legume and gas forms as part of the digestion process in the animals multiple stomachs. Some cows were more sensitive to bloat than others.

Once I saw that an animal was showing signs of bloat, a ballooning of their skin and heavy breathing, some action had to be taken. We found the least traumatic to the cow was to put a rope around her neck and lead her to a deep ditch where the cow could stand with her hind legs low and her front legs high. A combination of cold water from a hose on the cow's back and salt stuffed down her throat soon produced loud belching. Sometimes this procedure had to go on for forty-five minutes, but we never lost a valuable cow. I hated it happening because it always cut an hour from my work schedule.

About noon my father would arrive home from the delivery route. I would unload the truck and re-load it for an early afternoon delivery route to a much smaller town about eight miles in the direction opposite from Lodi. I would make that delivery and be back home shortly after 2:00 in the afternoon.

During late spring, summer and early fall days, haying operations went on simultaneously. My father would do most of the alfalfa hay cutting and raking. We both monitored the irrigation of the pastures, the alfalfa and the ten acres of winery grapes. My younger brothers continued with the milking part and helped haul in hay to the barn during summers and on weekends.

Every hour of each day wasn't all work. Occasionally I stole an hour to go to a big back-water pond, climb into my boat, and try to sneak up on frogs along the bank. I found that it was true that frogs would leap to grab a bit of red cloth on a triple fish hook.

If I caught several frogs, I cleaned and dressed them and saved them for an aunt and uncle. Sometimes my mother fried one for me.

I cost my father a lot of money one year, because I insisted I could do a job he had always done — that of ditching the vineyard to get ready for irrigation.

He told me what to do and exactly how deep to set the ditcher that was pulled behind a tractor.

Because the tractor wouldn't move fast enough to suit me, making nice, deep ditches, I changed the setting and got through the ditching job in a hurry.

The grapes didn't get near enough water during the summer using the shallow ditches and we ended up with half of a crop.

My father never made an issue of it but I was certain he knew what I had done.

* * * * *

I had my only bad experience with a car sometime during my first year following graduation.

Sports, Woodshop and Graduation

My father had purchased a new 1939 Chevrolet sedan-delivery to use for delivering bottled milk and also for family use when needed. It had a full-width front seat but no other seats. The car's front end was like any other sedan. The two rear doors opened so the entire space behind the front seat was usable. It was ideal for loading in the oak milk crates partitioned to hold a dozen quarts of milk.

Quite often I took my two younger brothers to high school if I were making the morning milk route that day.

It was cold with a light rain, and was probably winter time. We weren't more than two miles from home when I lost control of the milk truck. Maybe I had stepped on the brakes; maybe I turned the steering wheel abruptly. Whatever the cause I suddenly had no control of the steering. The milk truck slowly turned sideways on the county road, still moving about forty miles an hour. I remember saying to my brothers, "I can't steer it."

The next second the vehicle shot off the road. The rear end hit a tree in the orchard alongside the road, tearing off a rear fender. The car turned on its side. I can remember the frightening sound of a hundred glass milk bottles breaking as the car hit the tree, followed by more sickening sounds as the car tipped over.

My two brothers and I were cushioned by the back of the front seat as the car was moving backwards when it hit the tree. Likely none of us would have lived had we hit the tree moving forward and caught the force of the flying glass. There were no such things as seatbelts to stop us from going through the windshield.

We all crawled out through the driver's side window. I could see that Don's hand was bleeding badly. Harold and I were fine although badly scared.

There wasn't much traffic but those who drove by stopped to see what had happened. I convinced one motorist to take Don to a Lodi hospital so a doctor could take care of his bleeding hand. Harold and I walked the two miles home in the drizzle.

My parents saw us as we walked into the yard. My mother screamed when she realized Don wasn't with us. My father was angry and annoyed. How could I have possibly lost control and wrecked his milk truck? I had no answers and tried to defend myself as best I could. The rear tires had just slipped on the wet pavement.

My father said there was no alternative except that my car would become the milk delivery truck. This relieved my mind a little because that way I could contribute something to help with the damage I had caused.

Within an hour we had the rear seat removed and my car loaded with a new supply of milk. I set off again, still able to get Harold to school, though badly late. Somehow Don got home shortly afterwards. Perhaps the man who took him to the doctor also waited and brought him home. We didn't have a telephone because of the cost of stringing wires up our half-mile private lane, so my father went to the neighbors to call the insurance company and a tow truck. While I was completing the morning delivery he took the big farm truck and cleaned up the glass and recovered the oak milk crates. I don't believe a single bottle of milk was salvaged.

Loading and unloading my nice sedan as a "milk truck" was a real chore but I stuck with it for about ten days until the sedan delivery was repaired. My father and younger brother had the same inconvenience for the night milk route. For a long while afterwards on rainy days I kept waiting for the tires on the milk truck to again begin to slip and my having to relive that awful experience.

My sister, Yvonne, decided to drop out of high school during her sophomore year. It wasn't what I would have wanted for her and I don't remember her reasons.

I believe Yvonne had met a young Marine, a relative of one of the families who worked for a while on our dairy. It's possible they were talking about a serious relationship, even marriage.

* * * * *

We never went on a vacation, even once, during the dozen years I was involved in dairy work. Once I was out of school I suggested to my father that my brothers and I might take a short vacation once a year. I assured him there would be no lessening of farm and dairy work getting done. He wouldn't hear of it so I gave up talking about it. I didn't feel that my father was very wise in that decision, but it wasn't a major issue and didn't hurt our relationship.

I had visions of each of us being able to spend a week with one of our uncles and aunts, part of my mother's family.

Not only did the one uncle and aunt have the mountain lodge near Murpheys, but both had homes at Lake Tahoe.

I just knew they would invite us in a minute if they thought we were allowed to go.

Until my father turned the idea down cold, I built dreams of the jobs in the mountains my brothers and I could help our relatives with — wood cutting, cleaning up forest debris, painting — a vacation didn't need to be all play.

After Graduation

Most of my father's family continued to live in Humboldt County so we saw very little of them after moving to Lodi, in time for my fourth grade.

My mother's family, in contrast, all lived in the Lodi area. By the time Roy and I were in high school, two annual family events were something I looked forward to more than any other family visits.

One uncle had purchased or built a mountain cabin near a little town called Arnold. Getting there always meant passing through a larger town called Murpheys. After a long drive of almost two hours from our ranch, Murpheys was a welcome sight because it meant there was only an additional fifteen-minute drive.

Our uncle and aunt invited the entire family, about twenty people, for Thanksgiving Day each year. It was a wonderful event. By mid-afternoon everyone had arrived. We were always the last and the big main room, with a kitchen at one end and a huge fireplace at the other end, would already be filled with the smell of the turkey roasting.

My uncle would first show us his newest innovations, such as a ladder dropping from the ceiling to provide entrance to the attic bedroom. He was an engineer and delighted in constructing things that made their mountain retreat more livable. Two full-sized beds came out of the wall, but with no sign of them when put back into place.

My uncle had constructed a shooting range for the half dozen of us who liked target practice. To make sure the shooting was safe, the paper targets moved on a system of pulleys and an endless cable to a position against a tree about fifty feet from the shooting area. He provided a .22 rifle and encouraged us to shoot all we wanted to.

My older brother and a cousin always were top scorers in the shooting contest. I was never able to steady the rifle enough to consistently hit the inner target circles. It was a great challenge, though, and I never felt badly about not being a "winner."

Before leaving, each family would select and cut an evergreen tree for Christmas. These would be tied atop each vehicle for the trip home.

My family was always the first to leave following dinner. Not only was there a two-hour drive home, but the milking and related work followed. Most times we were finished by 10:00 P.M., and the milk delivery truck loaded. My father and younger brother seldom completed the Thanksgiving night delivery until after midnight. For everyone it was an exhausting day, but one that I, at least, was soon looking forward to again.

Christmas dinner, also centered around an immense turkey, was hosted by my mother's other brother and my aunt. It was a much shorter drive so didn't require as long a day for my family. The main meal was eaten in the early afternoon so my family could take care of the evening dairy work during our normal hours. Gifts weren't officially exchanged but we knew there would be envelopes under the tree with fifty cents or a dollar in each for us children.

My favorite part was the hour-long touch football game in the big yard following the turkey dinner. My oldest cousin, almost thirty by then, not only played well but acted as arbitrator for the inevitable arguments.

Our Lodi grandparents always were part of the family get-togethers at Thanksgiving and Christmas. My mother's life was so much happier with them close by.

When we lived for five years at the grade B dairy, they drove their well-kept Dodge sedan out to our place every month or two.

On the Fourth of July they always showed up with several packages of firecrackers. My mother was frightened at the thought of us boys blowing off our fingers with the powerful firecrackers, but she accepted her parents' wish to bring this excitement to us.

Our favorite activity was to light a firecracker under an empty canned fruit can. The challenge was to see how high we could blast the tin cans into the sky, often thirty feet or more.

Both grandparents died from separate home accidents or illnesses during the couple of years following my graduation from high school.

* * * * *

I had my own car to drive. If I wanted to go to a movie occasionally or go to the high school on a Sunday afternoon to play touch football with friends, my father gave me the freedom to use all the gasoline I needed. If I wanted to take one of the girls I knew to a movie and for a snack afterwards, he always gave me the several dollars I asked for.

From the time I was five or six I developed an ever-increasing admiration for my father's ability to build or fix things.

If a vehicle was stuck in a ditch during winter rains, in a very short while my father had a length of chain wrapped around the tire and through the spokes, and the car or truck came right out on it's own power.

When a flat tire occurred on the family car, in thirty minutes the tube had been patched, the tire mounted and inflated with a hand pump and off we went again.

Occasionally our car engine developed a "knock" on a day a trip was planned. Within two or three hours the oil pan had been "dropped," the bearings removed and examined, and "shims" added or removed, and our car engine ran smoothly once more.

My father became a master with a welding torch. On a farm, such an ability, along with a selection of strips of junk iron he meticulously saved, kept many a piece of farm machinery going. Otherwise, hours or days of work would be lost.

Sometime after my graduation from high school, my father said he was going to build a new house. He showed us a location where the house would be situated. My father said it could be built in six months with the help of one man, a good unemployed carpenter he knew of.

The two-bedroom house soon took shape with the forming and pouring of the concrete foundation. As I remember the only main part my brothers and I helped with was the digging of the pit for the septic tank and the forming work and pouring of the concrete for the walls, partitions and floors.

I did help my father for a few hours at a time nailing down the composition roof.

To my amazement the house was fully completed within the six months, with tongue-and-groove hardwood floors throughout.

In a way I had hoped we might move into this new house, especially since my mother had never lived in any but old homes in her married life.

This wasn't to be though. My father said it was built for any family we might hire to work on the ranch.

I'll never forget the near rage exhibited by my father one day months later when he stopped by his brand new house to talk with the hired man and saw the wife throw a full pail of soapy water on his beautiful hardwood floor, as a way of cleaning the room.

* * * * *

One day I arrived home with the skeleton of a fourteen-foot kayak tied to the top of my car. I had seen it advertised in the paper for $15 and had to have it. We had a city-operated park on a lake about five miles from our ranch. The lake was formed by water held back by an irrigation and flood-control dam on the river that circled our ranch. Several times I had visited the park and swam in the semi-clear water. When I saw the kayak advertised, I could just visualize myself skimming across the lake in my own kayak.

My father was less than pleased and said I couldn't keep it. I know he had immediate visions of my tipping the delicate boat and drowning. I set the boat aside for a few days while I measured it for a new canvas cover. The kayak had a fine frame made of aluminum ribs and hardwood longitudinal strips. I would have to construct seats.

Within three weeks I had a boat ready for the lake. Contrary to what dire predictions my friends made, I immediately became adept at stepping into my kayak without overturning it. I was amazed at the speed I could generate with the long double paddle that came with the boat.

My father relented and I heard no more about giving up my boat. It was a real treasure. I found that for fifty cents a month I could rent space on a rack at the lake. The park was closed and the gates locked at 11:00 P.M. during the summer. With a padlock and light chain to prevent my kayak from being removed from the rack, I felt confident about the security of my boat. Hardly a weekend went by but what I paddled around the lake, mostly with friends or one of my younger brothers.

No one ever suggested I was "macho"; the term may not have been invented by that time.

Somehow I got an idea, though, to paint six-inch high hearts on both sides of the front of my kayak. Any girl I took for a ride in my boat ended up with her initials lettered inside one of the hearts.

I had a lot of questions, but decided to give very few direct answers. Over the period of a couple of years, I accumulated a dozen or more sets of initials inside my painted hearts.

I tried to dodge the question of what it all meant, and probably wasn't sure myself.

* * * * *

After Graduation

With graduation over I became a full-time part of the dairy operation with my father while my younger brothers continued in high school.

One summer my father decided to develop a twenty-acre piece of "bottom-land" adjacent to the river into usable crop growing land. Up to then this piece of land was in natural grass, lots of wild rose bushes and a number of small oak trees. We used it almost entirely as a pasture for a dozen growing heifers not yet old enough for breeding and becoming part of the milking herd.

I had used the field with the brambles and small trees as a prime hunting ground for cottontail rabbits. One nice cottontail made a fine change of meat for dinner. The small animals came out of their hiding places just before dusk to feed. I could grab my rifle right after milking and have thirty minutes to hunt before it became too dark.

It was a major family project to dig out and burn the huge patches of wild rose bushes. The roots had to be dug out and also piled for burning. The dozen trees were not nearly the miserable task to remove as were the bushes.

We must have worked several months, using all available time not needed to keep the dairy going. It was tough to keep enthusiastic, even with the reward ahead of having additional land for irrigated pastures or to rent out for crops such as tomatoes.

The final leveling and grading was done by a professional person with heavy equipment who my father hired to do the work.

Many more days were needed to mix and pour concrete and lay pipes to bring irrigation water to the newly developed piece of land. I learned a lot about using surveying equipment. I also threw thousands of shovelfulls of small rocks, sand and cement into our little gasoline powered mixer to make concrete for the project.

I missed the cottontail hunting. It had been fairly easy to use one of the heifers as cover and slowly sneak into a good position for a clear shot.

We never completed the concrete ditches and "gates" to carry water across the newly-developed field. My father reluctantly gave in to my argument that above-ground concrete flumes were preferable to underground pipes.

After hundreds of hours of building forms for the flumes and mixing and pouring concrete, I realized how wrong I had been. My father was off doing other stuff and didn't interfere.

I was trying to save us a few dollars and cost us a season of crops.

* * * * *

About noon on December 7, 1941, I had just completed my milk delivery at the final store, collected the money and purchased the few grocery items to take home. When I turned on the milk truck radio, every bit of news was about the Japanese having just bombed Pearl Harbor.

Everything seemed to change quickly after that event. Much of the change likely would have been made anyway. Demands of the dairy business were different than when my parents chose to buy out the two small raw milk dairies. Raw milk was going out of favor and pasteurization requirements were almost certain. More people wanted to buy homogenized milk.

With a small dairy of around thirty-five cows, my father didn't see how he could possibly justify the expensive equipment needed to move into pasteurization and homogenization. He was no doubt right. We had discussed the changing market many times in recent months. I had no argument as I knew our position wasn't strong.

It wasn't long before my father said he had reached a number of decisions. We were going to discontinue the delivery of bottled raw milk. All of our milk, in bulk, was to be delivered daily and sold to a larger dairy in Lodi, a former major competitor. My father said he had talked with the owner and the deal had been agreed to. My father was to send out announcements to our customers that included a suggestion they continue with this new supplier.

In some ways I felt a wonderful sense of relief. There would be no more tight delivery schedules to meet. There would be no more bottles to wash and fill. The milk could go through the filtering and chilling process and right into ten-gallon cans, already cleaned and sterilized by the company buying our milk.

One other decision my father announced was that he was going to join a "Lodi Militia" that was being formed to help protect California from a possible invasion by the Japanese. They were to leave within a week for training in our mountains nearby.

My father said it would be necessary that I, along with my mother, be in charge of running the dairy. He took me to his bank and arranged for me to be able to sign all checks and to make deposits. I felt really grown up as we walked into the bank and put signatures on the necessary papers. Although I had had a lot of responsibility for the previous several years, now, just turning twenty, I felt awfully grown up. I felt rewarded, too, because it proved that my father trusted me with his money.

The "military thing" for my father lasted only a brief time. Whether the idea had been discarded and the unit disbanded, or whether my father had a change of mind, I can't remember, but he was home.

The war was well underway in Europe. My mother was worried because my older brother, Roy, had been taken by the Army's military draft and was in training at Fort Lewis, Washington.

My father must have been getting restless. He talked about the money that could be made catching a certain type of shark off the Pacific Coast. He saw, too, that being a supplier of this shark's liver oil could be a way of helping in the military effort.

I laughed about the idea because my father was always positive about wanting to have his "feet planted on dry land." Until he announced that he had lined up a forty-five foot fishing trawler in Monterey, I couldn't believe it was happening. Very shortly my father was gone. My mother, two younger brothers and I were left to operate the farm.

At some point my older brother, Roy, and Don, succumbed to the pleas of my father to join in his shark fishing venture. They, too, must have believed there were fortunes to be made from the sale of sharks' livers.

Roy had been released from the army training due to a medical hernia problem, and was now free to do as he chose. I didn't want any part of a life bouncing around on the ocean waves, handling smelly fish bait.

I confess I did listen with some envy about the bravery of fighting dragging anchors and heavy seas.

Girls and A Kayak

Once I was out of high school and became a full-time worker on our dairy, I naturally lost contact with most of the students still in school, especially the girls.

I had an occasional "kayak" or movie date with girls I met through my sister, who was also still living at home.

My afternoon milk route to the small town of Thornton, located several miles west of Lodi, brought me into contact with a few girls.

I developed a pretty close friendship with the son of a store owner who purchased milk from us. He and I had some pleasant weekend afternoons with girls he knew.

Writing letters became important to me because one girl I had known briefly, a friend of Lonzo's family, had moved to Texas with her mother who was divorced. I thought she was a really exciting girl and I knew she liked me.

Sometime around the time I was nineteen or twenty, Jodi and I were exchanging letters almost every month.

I don't remember whether I thought much about going steady with any of the girls where casual dates were involved. We didn't have a telephone on the ranch so girls couldn't call me even if they wished to. My only calls were made by going the half-mile to a neighbor's house.

Too often my limited number of evening dates almost became disasters before they started. Our cows needed a regular amount of time to eat dry alfalfa hay each night after being milked. Their heads were locked into stantions during that period.

After bathing (we did not have a shower) and dressing I would stop at the feeding barn, open the big sliding door and then unlock each of the stantions to release the animals. I could carefully walk between the animals and unlock two at a time.

Too often as I walked behind an animal to go between the next pair, she would step slightly backwards in anticipation of being released and her hoof would slip into the manure-filled concrete gutter.

My shirt, my trousers, my face, or all three would be spattered with fresh cow manure! Anyone who has had this happen knows how awful and permanent a smell this leaves.

It meant returning to the house, getting a fresh shirt from my mother, or washing out the green stain and smell from my clothes. Hopefully, if I ran my car heater, my clothes would be dry by the time I reached my date's home.

I had an uneasy feeling that I perpetually smelled like fresh cow dung. It may have been a factor in my not having very many repeat dates, though that didn't occur to me at the time.

Occasionally I stopped briefly to talk with a girl in Thornton who I thought was really friendly and pretty. She had a little black dog. One afternoon while I was standing beside the milk truck visiting with Ada, her little dog ran out into the street and was struck by a car. The little animal wasn't killed, but one eye was popped out from the blow and it's head seemed pretty badly damaged. Ada cried and pleaded with me to do something to help her pet.

I could think of nothing I could do to help the whimpering, bloody little animal except to rush it to a veterinarian. Unfortunately the nearest vet was in Lodi, over fifteen miles away. I could tell by Ada's eyes that she thought I was rather special to do that. Though totally blinded, the dog recovered completely otherwise, and would always come up to sniff me and be petted when I stopped to see Ada.

Our visits were always outside Ada's little house, located back off the street under some big oak trees. Her mother often wasn't home as she worked in the cannery located a few blocks from their house. If I saw her father, I don't remember. I believe he lived there, but may have been ill or disabled.

I guess my letters to Jodi in Texas became rather romantic. When I expected a letter back from her, I couldn't wait for someone else to bring in the mail, but would make a quick trip to the mailbox a half-mile away to see if she had written. My feelings for Jodi were strong though I didn't let on to my family, but she was in Texas anyway.

I had nice feelings about Ada in Thornton, also, and was quite sure she was glad to see me whenever I saw her on occasional drives to her little town. One day I got up courage to ask her if I might see her the following Saturday night after all of my chores were completed.

It was a really nice evening for me though I don't remember where we went or what we did. I did ask Ada if we could go steady. She seemed as excited as I was with this new relationship. She had a wonderful voice and sang "Maria Elena" to me as we sat in the car before saying goodnight. I drove home with a head full of mixed emotions. On one hand I was amazed that a beautiful girl could love me so much. On the other hand I shivered at the thought of what I had gotten myself into. We had agreed that I would see Ada the following Saturday after I had completed my part of the dairy work.

It had to have been only the next day or so that one of Lonzo's brothers came by to tell me that Jodi was driving with her mother from Texas to visit them. They were to arrive in about two weeks. The boy said he thought the purpose was so Jodi and I could be married! I didn't sleep much that night.

By the weekend I had reached a decision as to what action I would take. I would lie to both girls. I would tell Ada that I hadn't been exactly honest with her and that another girl was arriving shortly with the understanding that she was my fiancé.

Then when Jodi arrived I would tell her that things had changed and there was another girl I was going steady with.

It was a bad experience for me but not nearly as awful as it was for Ada and Jodi. Along with my loss, I did have a feeling of "escape."

Ada couldn't believe me. She didn't sing me any songs. She just sobbed the entire time we sat in my car.

After Jodi arrived I took her for an evening ride on Lodi Lake in my kayak. We talked about everything but our thoughts for the future. After the kayak was stored and locked on its rack and we were in the car, I told Jodi her part of the lie. I can't remember how she took the news. She was tougher than Ada.

I never saw or wrote to either girl again. I just wondered over and over again how I could have treated two wonderful girls so awfully.

My own loss didn't hit me for several days. I was concentrating so hard on how to extricate myself from a situation of having two serious girlfriends that I totally overlooked where I would lose out.

After a few days and Jodi's departure, I wanted so badly to resume my friendship with Ada. I either didn't figure out how to take that step, or lacked the courage to do so. Nor did I ever share the information with anyone.

* * * * *

My two younger brothers, Don and Harold, proved to have all of the woodworking skills that I had, and more.

When it came time to select a woodshop project my father said the thing he needed most of all was a big walk-in ice box. The refrigerated compartment of the combined unit that chilled brine for pumping through the stainless steel milk chiller, was fully adequate to hold up to two dozen twelve-quart milk crates. The storage area was less than waist-high, though, and required lots of bent-over reaching and stacking. Perhaps my father was thinking of expanding the dairy.

I couldn't believe my brothers would take on such a huge project. Nor could I believe that Mr. Crose would approve it. Both however happened, and I asked each day how the building was coming.

It had to be a full-year project and maybe extended into a second year. I remember clearly when my father met my brothers at school and loaded the walk-in box onto our big truck.

It was a magnificent structure. The inside dimensions must have been six feet by eight feet and six and a half feet high. All of the walls, floor and ceiling were made with tongue-and-groove planks. The insulation between the inside and outside walls was ten inches thick. It was a structurally finished project, but like my boat and desk, arrived home unpainted. Time, again, had run out, but I had a great admiration for the precision and magnitude of the job my two brothers had accomplished.

My father never took the next step to equip the walk-in box for use on our dairy to store milk. It would have required buying and installing a suitable compressor unit. Maybe too much expense was involved; more likely, my father was losing interest in fighting a diminishing business.

The big box became a temporary storage place for expensive alfalfa and clover seed. When the huge hinged door was closed and the handle pulled down, it was truly the only mouse-proof place on our ranch. Many admiring friends just had to swing open the insulated door to see what my brothers had built.

With the bottling and home delivery of milk no longer a part of our dairy routine, each day moved along with less pressure. We milked the cows twice daily. Feeding was done, barns cleaned and the equipment scrubbed and sterilized.

My next younger brother, Don, had left high school before graduation and worked full-time with me during milking and mid-day hours.

Alfalfa hay had to be cut, cured and hauled to the big barn. Other than irrigation and early-morning sulfur dusting for mildew, our small vineyard required only occasional work.

Elimination of the three milk routes represented the greatest change. Now we could take a more leisurely approach to irrigation of pasture and alfalfa fields. No longer did we need to run from one job to another.

At some point my father apparently convinced my brothers Roy and Don to join him and be his crew on the shark-fishing boat. The project must have lasted several months. They had little success in catching sharks, but stayed with the boat. They were all proving to be good sailors, and had stories about riding out severe weather without serious problems, though scared.

My mother was totally supportive of our efforts to keep the dairy going. Each morning I would haul the filled cans of milk to town, pick up empty cans, and purchase any grocery items my mother needed. Our total income very likely was reduced by more than fifty percent when the bottle delivery was dropped. We laughed about our bare ability now to pay all of the bills.

My mother said she thought it was a good idea when I told her I wanted to purchase a new wheel tractor with a hay-mowing attachment. I was rather amazed when the equipment company didn't question our ability to make the $100 monthly payments. I believe we paid only $100 down on the $700 tractor.

Up until that time we had used a mowing machine designed and put together by my father. He had used an old engine and chassis from a car. The cutting sickle attached to the side had been part of a horse-drawn mower. A system of pulleys and belts and hand levers added up to a very suitable piece of farm machinery for several years.

It had, however, become increasingly difficult to start the engine, and to keep the mechanical parts of the mower operating. Because he was a good mechanic and welder, these were but minor inconveniences and of little concern to my father.

For me, any breakdown often stopped a full day's work as I could fix only minor problems. The new tractor with its attached mower made my life a lot more pleasant. I felt like a king when setting off to do a job with it.

There proved to be enough income from the bulk milk deliveries to make the $100 monthly payments on the new tractor.

I occasionally thought about learning to weld so I could repair broken equipment parts. I was certain my father would teach me. It never seemed the right time to ask.

I had confidence in my skills at a number of important activities on our farm. I could dig post holes, set posts accurately and stretch barbed wire fences as well as any man.

Laying water pipes of galvanized metal and threading the pipe ends so everything fit and didn't leak wasn't difficult.

I could load loose alfalfa hay on our big truck and trailer so the load wouldn't slip on the way to the barn. I really felt awfully good about what I could do.

* * * * *

The kayak was a significant part of my recreation for at least two years. It was always ready and waiting on its rack at the lake when I wanted to use it. As many as a dozen times I took girls I knew for evening moonlight rides on the lake. The curfew horn blasted out at 10:00 P.M., announcing the lake's closure to boating. It may not have been too exciting or pleasant for my "dates" as my big double paddle occasionally threw water on them. Also seating space in the narrow kayak didn't permit turning around. I sat in the rear compartment and my rider in the front one, with their back to me. Conversation was awkward.

One fall day I had taken my boat out for a spin and was about to lock it on the rack when three boys asked if they might use it. I hadn't remembered seeing any of the three before. I knew immediately that I was in a tight spot. The last thing I wanted was to have someone else using my prized but fragile canvas-covered kayak.

The boys were persistent though, and a greater concern was what they might do to my boat if I refused. Finally one said, "We'll give you fifty cents and will promise to take good care of it." I could see no alternative but to accept the fifty cents. I tried to be as friendly as I could and asked that they remember to lock my boat on its rack when they finished.

It wasn't until the following weekend that I was able to check out my kayak. My worst fears had been realized. There were a dozen foot-long knife slashes in the canvas. I sadly tied it on the top of my car and took it home, hoping someday to re-canvas it. That never happened.

Not having the kayak did give me some extra time to build something I knew my mother always wanted, a really nice front yard so visitors didn't have to come in through the back door. It embarrassed her to have people need to dodge piles of chicken manure before they could step up on the back porch to enter.

I knew my mother would like the finished front yard and entryway that I visualized. A lot of "forming" and pouring concrete was needed for a base on which to build the fence. It proved to be a beautiful white-painted fence, made of one-by-four inch boards, with two arched gates.

Time ran out before I could put in the walkways or work up the ground and plant the lawn. My mother assured me that she really loved what I had done, though both of us knew it would end up being never completed or used.

A Vacation; I Become A Sailor

Once the Japanese bombed Pearl Harbor, more and more of my friends enlisted or were drafted into the armed forces. Every issue of our daily newspaper carried pictures of our community's young men who were answering the call of our nation. Occasionally one of the girls I dated would ask if I were going to go into the armed forces. Some of them wanted to be nurses.

I can't remember what brought on my decision. It could have been a feeling of being "left out." Maybe I wanted to prove I could be a military man as well as any of the others. It would be an "escape" from the endless dairy work. I had been out of high school almost three years. There was no possible way for me to make any money. I had made a $5 bet with a doubting adult acquaintance that I would go on to college after helping my parents on our dairy for a few years. That likelihood looked dim.

One morning I announced to my mother and father that I was going to celebrate my twenty-first birthday by taking a week-long vacation. I then jolted them by telling them I was also planning to enlist in the US Coast Guard. I had two weeks to get the required three letters of recommendation from non-related people.

All of the men I asked for the character recommendations said they would be glad to do that. One was the dairy owner where we were delivering our bulk milk. The second was the minister of the church my family occasionally attended. A longtime friend of my father was the third person. He was the owner of the vineyards where my father, brothers and I had burned grape prunings when I was nine or ten.

I would listen to none of the pleas of my parents to reconsider my decision to enlist. My mother was saddened and apprehensive over the possibility of losing all of her four sons to the military. One already had been drafted (though now had a medical discharge), here I was going and my two younger brothers, now seventeen and nineteen, couldn't be very far behind.

My father couldn't see how I could possibly want to get involved in the war. He was certain he could get a deferment for me because of the necessity to keep our country's farms operating. I wasn't listening to any arguments.

* * * * *

I had decided on where to go on this first vacation. My first stop would be my aunt and uncle's home in Eureka, in Humboldt County. Next would be a drive along the Pacific Ocean and two days with another aunt and uncle and cousins on their big mountain ranch. The final two-day stop was planned to be at my grandfather's campground and the chance to see our old ranch for the first time since we had left it.

At the start of the trip I stopped in San Francisco and signed up for enlistment in the Coast Guard. Their next "boot camp" contingent wouldn't be until June which meant I would have another three or four months before actual enlistment.

My relatives were glad to see me after so many years. February is almost always cold and rainy in that north country, and this was no exception. The first two stops were all visiting, eating and sleeping. I do recall almost freezing during my first stop. My cousin, about eighteen, was a "fresh air freak." Our bedroom was on the second floor of their home. The bed we shared was next to a wide open window and the cold, damp air poured in on us all night. I was glad to get up in the morning for a warm breakfast.

I was really disappointed to find my grandparents not home. It was their custom to take trips at least once each year and I had selected that week. Eventually I located a man who was acting as caretaker during my grandparents' absence. He agreed to open up a cabin for me. There were no other occupants in any of the summer cabins. I had the entire place to myself. It wasn't what I wanted.

I remember the days being sunny though cold. I couldn't wait to climb the hill behind our old home. It didn't seem nearly as steep as I had fixed in my memory, nor as far to the "second opening." I sneaked throughout the final group of evergreens, hoping to find a grazing deer.

I jumped from rock to rock as I worked my way upstream in the little creek where my brother, Roy, and I spent so many wonderful hours. There was more water, but no rain for several days had left the water clear.

My grandparents were still using the same water system that I had remembered. A tank halfway down the hill now collected water for the summer campers. I felt good about reaching the source of the water and cleaning the debris from the screen placed at the pipe opening.

I froze both nights. The cabins were built for summer occupancy. There was plenty of firewood and I made sure the cabin was warm and a load of wood in the little stove before going to bed. By two or three in the morning the cabin was cold and I was cold. I would rebuild a fire, wait until the cabin warmed, and then climb back into bed. By morning I was chilled again.

Eating was a disaster. I drove to the little store three miles from the campground and bought a loaf of bread and some cheese. I may have bought a can of spaghetti, some cereal and milk, and maybe a few eggs. Whatever it was, it was cold and left me with a feeling I hadn't eaten. I couldn't wait to leave.

Our routine at the dairy resumed as if I hadn't left for my week's vacation. I felt good knowing I was helping again on our dairy, but with something positive ahead for me.

* * * * *

Early in June I arrived in San Francisco by bus for induction into the Coast Guard. The recruitment people told me I still needed to wait a week but that they would put me up at a hotel and provide "meal tickets" during my wait.

I wandered around the part of San Francisco near my hotel looking ahead to what was certain to be a long week. On the spur of the moment I asked an employee at a White Log Coffee Shop, one of several in the city, if I might get a job for the week. To my surprise the manager

A Vacation, I Become A Sailor

said they needed a dishwasher and someone to scrub down the restaurant at closing.

That very afternoon I began work at 4:00 and worked until 2:00 A.M. I wasn't used to those kind of hours, but was delighted to be busy and making more money than I ever had in my life.

On the final night at the restaurant I was asked to wait on several tables because the waitress was extra busy.

One young Naval officer had two young women with him. They ordered our best dinner, a small steak. When I collected for the dinners, the officer handed me a dime tip, with a very profound statement, "You can use this more than I, where I'm going." Never would I have dreamed that in just over two years, I, too, would be a naval officer heading back into the Pacific war zone!

* * * * * * * * * * * * * * * * * * * *

It was with mixed emotions that I climbed into the upper bunk of the barracks on Government Island in Alameda that first night as a Coast Guardsman, and listened to taps. How would I handle myself? Where would I go? What new experiences would I have? Where would it all end?